Village ‘

—— in —

MIDDLESEX &
WEST LONDON

Village Walks in MIDDLESEX & WEST LONDON

David Hall and Rosemary Hall

COUNTRYSIDE BOOKS
NEWBURY BERKSHIRE

COUNTRYSIDE BOOKS
3 Catherine Road
Newbury, Berkshire

ISBN 1 85306 501 3

Designed by Graham Whiteman
Photographs by the authors
Maps by Rosemary Hall
Illustrations by Trevor Yorke

Front cover photo of Enfield
taken by John Bethell

Produced through MRM Associates Ltd., Reading
Typeset by Techniset Typesetters, Newton-le-Willows
Printed by Woolnough Bookbinding Ltd., Irthlingborough

Contents

INTRODUCTION

WALK

1   LALEHAM $(1^3/_4$ or $4^3/_4$ miles)   10

2   SHEPPERTON $(4^1/_2$ miles)   15

3   SUNBURY $(3^3/_4$ miles)   19

4   NORWOOD $(3$ miles)   23

5   HANWELL $(4^1/_2$ miles)   27

6   EALING GREEN $(2^1/_4$ miles)   31

7   HAREFIELD $(6$ miles)   35

8   SOUTH HAREFIELD $(5^1/_2$ miles)   39

9   RUISLIP $(2^3/_4$ miles)   44

10   PINNER $(4$ miles)   49

11   HARROW $(3^1/_2$ miles)   53

12   NORTHOLT $(7$ miles)   57

13   STANMORE $(3^3/_4$ miles)   61

14   ARKLEY $(4^3/_4$ miles)   65

AREA MAP SHOWING LOCATION OF THE WALKS

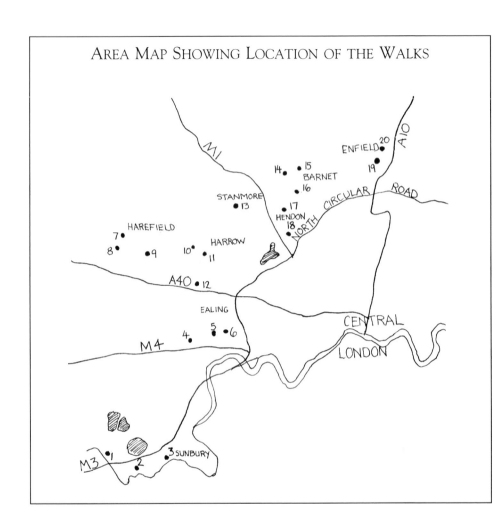

WALK

15	MONKEN HADLEY *(3 miles)*	69
16	TOTTERIDGE *(3 miles)*	74
17	MILL HILL *(4¹/₂ miles)*	78
18	HENDON *(5 miles)*	84
19	ENFIELD CHASE *(3 miles)*	89
20	ENFIELD – FORTY HALL *(3¹/₂ miles)*	94

To our parents, and
Kimberley and Holly

Publisher's Note

We hope that you obtain considerable enjoyment from this book; great care has been taken in its preparation. Although at the time of publication all routes followed public rights of way or permitted paths, diversion orders can be made and permissions withdrawn.

We cannot of course be held responsible for such diversion orders and any inaccuracies in the text which result from these or any other changes to the routes, nor any damage which might result from walkers trespassing on private property. However, we are anxious that all details covering the walks are kept up to date and would therefore welcome information from readers which would be relevant to future editions.

Introduction

London is a collection of villages. How many times do you hear that? How often do you think that it is still true as you dodge the traffic in the busy High Street of one of those villages?

We have been out in the old county of Middlesex to find circular walks around the hearts of the villages that went to make up Greater London. It has been an absolute pleasure. An astonishing number of these villages have managed to keep some parts of the traditional core of village green, church, pub, cluster of unpretentious houses and the odd manor house and mansion. Sometimes, just yards away from a busy road, concealed by a row of modern shop fronts, a group of timber-framed buildings will shelter a mediaeval parish church. A quiet side road will lead you to an unexpected village green overlooked by the pub and church.

Of course, in the outer fringes of the county, some of the villages are still in open countryside, and you would expect to be able to walk out of the village into fields and woods. But would you expect to stroll out of a peaceful churchyard into a great meadow that was part of a working farm not so very many years ago in the centre of Hendon? The built-up areas have a surprising amount of green open spaces for walks; fields of city farms purchased by public-spirited councils, parkland that once belonged to the houses of high society, parcels of common land, remnants of ancient royal hunting forest, stretches of preserved wilderness hugging the banks of the many streams and minor rivers that snake through the county.

Development itself has created features of the landscape that make interesting walks. Middlesex had to be crossed by anyone wanting to reach London from the North and West, so it has had more than its share of the industrial revolution's lines of communication scored through it. We have put some of these to good use. Several of the walks run beside canals, along disused railway lines, or by lakes that were formed by gouging out gravel for motorways and are now wildfowl reserves.

The urbanised villages of Middlesex have a special flavour of their own. Their London Boroughs can afford to maintain footpaths and their signposts properly; they can run free museums and keep up grand houses like Forty Hall and Pitshanger Manor. And where else could you amble up a hill to admire an apparently isolated little mediaeval church, and stroll down the other side to view the largest mosque in Europe?

All the chapters tell you how to get to the walk route by car and give advice on parking, but we went to them all by public transport and include details of nearby stations. If, however, you decide to drive please ensure that you park in such a way as not to be a nuisance to those who live nearby.

A prime objective has been to provide clear route descriptions for each walk, coupled with an easily-followed sketch map. For those requiring more detail – including the main features of views – the numbers of the relevant OS Pathfinder 1:25 000 maps are given; many of the routes are additionally covered by a

London street atlas (Nicholson's or A to Z), which is easy to carry and names the roads.

A place offering food and drink – more often than not a local pub – has also been suggested for each walk. Opening times and specific menu details have not been included as they can often change. These can, of course, always be obtained by using the telephone number at the end of each description.

We should like to thank all the people who smoothed our path, including many nameless (to us) staff of local libraries and museums, tenants and bar staff of the pubs and places of refreshment, Valerie Payne of the church bell-ringers (who watched over David's attempts to chime the 5-cwt bell of St Mary's in Norwood) and, especially, the people of Middlesex, The Middle Saxons, who provided so much friendly help, advice and invaluable local knowledge of their own villages.

David Hall and Rosemary Hall

LALEHAM

Length : 1³/₄ or 4³/₄ miles

Getting there: Leave the M3 at Sunbury and head west on the A308; turn left onto the A244 through Upper Halliford, then turn right onto the B3366 (B376) past Shepperton station and on to Laleham. Railtrack: Staines is 1 mile from point 7 (along Kingston Road, then footpath down the side of Matthew Arnold School).	Parking: By Laleham Park, and at the riverside. If leaving your car in Laleham Park start the walk at point 2. From the riverside car park, walk through the trees past the toilet block and, again, start at point 2.	Maps: OS Pathfinder 1190 Weybridge, Esher & Hampton Court and (for a short section) 1174 Staines, Heathrow Airport & Richmond (GR 051689).

Laleham's history has its intriguing aspects. It seems respectable and worthy enough: it has a number of pleasant Georgian and early Victorian buildings and very fine parkland at the old centre, is still surrounded by open country and has a very attractive riverside. Penton Hook Island, just upstream, is where the narrator

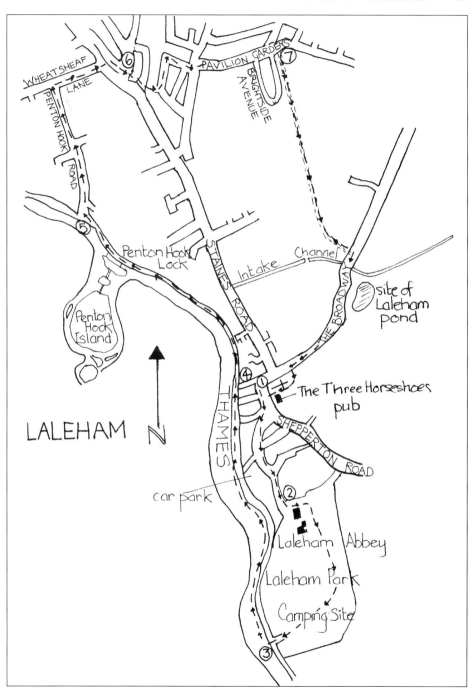

The riverside at Laleham.

of *Three Men in a Boat* wanted to stop for the night. Thomas Arnold taught here before becoming headmaster of Rugby. His son Matthew is buried here. However, there are fascinating stories beneath the surface of Laleham, like the tunnel said to connect the church and the pub. Edward VIII entertained Lillie Langtry at the Three Horseshoes, which is still said to be a place where lovers meet. A musical comedy star, Marie Studholme, had a house built here in 1909 by Edward Maufe (the architect of Guildford cathedral). All of this adds a certain savour to the charm of the village.

Laleham is the family seat of the Binghams, the Earls of Lucan. Laleham House, surrounded by fine grounds, was built for the 2nd Earl in 1803. The 3rd Lord Lucan ordered the Charge of the Light Brigade in the Crimean War. The 5th Lord Lucan sold off Laleham House to a religious community in 1928, when it became known as Laleham Abbey (it has since changed hands again and is now

---

FOOD and DRINK

The Three Horseshoes is an old coaching inn dating back at least to the 17th-century. Still allegedly a place for assignations, this is where Edward VIII met Lillie Langtry. It is certainly very popular at lunchtime, not just amongst clandestine lovers. There are numerous places to sit and eat, or just drink, indoors and out. The food is excellent and plentiful, and of course, you can always say that you were treated like royalty. Telephone: 01784 452617.

All Saints church, Laleham.

private residences). The 7th Lord Lucan went missing in 1974, following the murder of his children's nanny. The 3rd, 4th and 5th Earls are buried in the family vault behind the church. The 7th Earl is still apparently lord of the manor. Wherever he is.

Begin at the end of Blacksmith's Lane, home to the local forge and an imposing Regency mansion. Near the church is Dial House, a local 18th-century landmark bearing a prominent sundial. You next pass some more of the fine 18th and 19th-century buildings, before circling the parkland round Laleham Abbey. Then walk along the river nearly into Staines, pass near a school named for Matthew Arnold and continue through countryside to the

churchyard where he is buried. If you just want to do the shorter walk, you leave the riverside path at point 4, Blacksmith's Lane, to return to the church.

THE WALK

❶   Start by the war memorial, facing the church. Take a look at Blacksmith's Lane, leading towards the river, and the houses to the left of the church, then head to the right, passing the church, then Dial House, on Shepperton Road. Turn right opposite the Three Horseshoes onto Ferry Lane. Fork left into Abbey Drive, passing The Coverts, of the early 1700s, and a picturesque thatched cottage. Pass the public toilet and approach the gateway to Laleham Abbey.

❷   Turn left onto the parkland and walk round the central fenced-off private property. Go past some very fine cedar trees, then keep to the outer perimeter, passing a sports field on your right. Leave the park to get to the river.

❸   Turn right and walk back along the riverside, cloaked with willow trees. The swans here seem to be getting outnumbered by Canada geese. Pass the car park and the end of Ferry Lane. At the end of Condor Road, on the corner, is The Barn, Marie Studholme's house. Follow the Thames Path signs along the riverside.

❹   At the end of Blacksmith's Lane, you can take a (very) short cut up the lane back to the starting point. Otherwise continue along the riverside. Penton Hook Lock gives access to Penton Hook Island via walkways on the lock gates – the island is an attractive nature reserve worth a small diversion. After the lock, keep on the riverside path as far as the road on the right by the corner postbox in the wall, opposite a double signpost ('Laleham 1, Staines $1^1/_2$').

❺   Turn right down this avenue, Penton Hook Road. Pass the end of Penton Hall Drive on the left. Turn right at the T junction with Wheatsheaf Lane, then cross the main Laleham Road. Turn right and follow the main road along the quieter parallel residential road beyond the reservation. Pass the end of Grosvenor Road.

❻   After the Laleham boundary sign and the following lamppost, turn left onto a narrow alleyway. At the end, follow the road round to the left. Veer right at the end, and exit Lansdowne Road onto the main Worple Road. Turn left and first right into Pavilion Gardens.

❼   Just before the primary school, turn right into the alleyway by the side of the school (if you turned left here, you would pass the playing fields of the Matthew Arnold School). After the end of the playing field, the path passes between meadows and is lined by shrubbery. The path becomes a lane; go through a wooden kissing gate and walk down the lane to turn right at the main Ashford Road. Cross the water channel – opposite the restaurant is Laleham Pond (being restored at the time of writing as a natural habitat). Pass a group of old farm buildings on the right, then a couple of Laleham's pubs. Enter the churchyard, go round the church, passing the large Lucan monument, to leave by the front lychgate.

WALK 2
SHEPPERTON
Length : 4¹/₂ miles

Getting there: Leave the M3 at Sunbury and head west on the A308, turning left onto the A244 through Upper and Lower Halliford; at the roundabout, turn right onto the B375, then turn left at the next roundabout into Church Road. Railtrack: Shepperton.

Parking: Manor Park, off Church Road. You would then start the walk at point 2. The village square has very few parking spaces.

Map: OS Pathfinder 1190 Weybridge, Esher & Hampton Court (GR 077666).

Shepperton's old centre is very picturesque, with the traditional grouping of church, rectory and pub round a village square. There is also a passenger ferry that is still operating. Funnily enough, this tradition is allied to a long involvement with science fiction. H.G. Wells describes in great detail its destruction by his Martians in *The War of the Worlds*, the writer J.G. Ballard has lived here for decades, and the *Alien* first began its stalking of Sigourney Weaver at the nearby film studios.

H.G. Wells' Martians notwithstanding, the village square is still one of the most attractive in Middlesex. You then walk

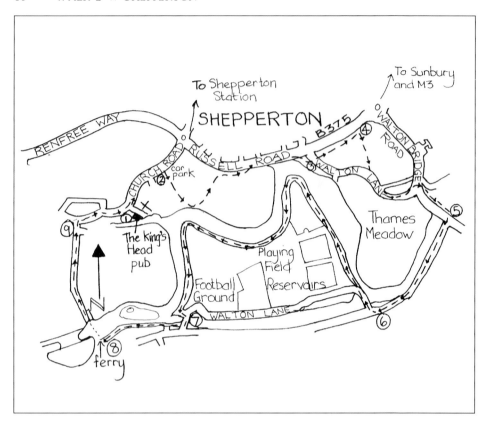

through Manor Park, which contains good mature trees, to the river, and continue through more woods and open space to cross the river at Walton Bridge. You return along the Surrey side, following the natural course of the Thames along the artificial Desborough Island. You complete the circle by returning on one of the few passenger ferries remaining on the river. This is supported by the Environment Agency as it links sections of the Thames Path. However, before starting, it may be a good idea to make sure it is running normally (contact Nauticalia Boats on 01932 254844).

THE WALK

❶ From the village square, visit the church and riverside, then leave the river, pass the church and turn right onto Church

---

FOOD and DRINK

The King's Head, with a wonderful position on the square, is a very popular traditional pub with flagstone floors in the bars, serving Courage, Theakston and Ruddles ales and a good range of food. Lots of small bars and nooks and crannies are available in which to enjoy your drink and people-watch; actors from the nearby Shepperton Studios have been known to step inside for refreshment. Telephone: 01932 221910.

Manor Park.

Road, following it round to the right.

❷ Turn right at Manor Park car park, following a Thames Path Alternative Route sign. Walk down a drive at the right of the park. Fork right at the end; leave the park on a bridleway-standard track between a fence and wall. Turn right at the end of the wall, then left at the river to walk along the bank. Firstly, follow the river, behind the trees, then veer left, crossing a ditch. Go half left through the next meadow, and cross a sleeper bridge. The footpath, clearly marked by wooden kerbs, passes through thickets, with a cricket ground on the left. Walk through a car park, then, just before the height barrier, turn right onto another clearly-marked path. You have woods on

your right and Russell Road on the left. Take the wheelchair-accessible bridge up to the level of the road and continue past the Ship Hotel and Red Lion.

❸ Just before Walton Lane, turn half right onto a footpath and cross the lane, following the Thames Path signs. Keep straight on, following the right side of the broad green. Nearly at the end, a public footpath marked by rows of stakes crosses your route.

❹ Turn right here, follow another Thames Path sign and enter a large, neatly-mown open space. Follow the path out onto the road, turn left and follow the road to Walton Bridge. Cross Walton Bridge

Road (the only footpath is on the left) and go over the river.

❺   Leave the bridge down the steps at the left, turn left at the river and go under the bridge. Come to Desborough Island and a first bridge. You are on the Surrey river bank, but the engineering work that formed Desborough Island in 1935 was part-financed by the old Middlesex Council.

Parts of the walk in point 6 round the island are quite secluded. Some walkers may prefer to stay on the straight path along the channel as far as the second bridge and rejoin the directions at point 7.

❻   Climb the steps to the bridge, cross the channel, then turn right off the vehicle track onto the footpath. Follow this path round the perimeter of the island. At first you get only glimpses of the river, but Point Meadow Open Space gives a good view of the river, then, after some willow trees, the path veers left at the edge of the island and you have a good view of the old centre of Shepperton, the manor house on the right and the Warren Lodge Hotel on the left. Continue on round the edge of the island, passing meadows with long grass on your left, until the path climbs to cross the second bridge. Turn right down the steps and rejoin the Thames Path.

❼   Continue upstream, passing the foot-bridge to the private Eyot House. Just beyond this is a set of steps on the right down to the river, with a sign for the ferry, which runs half-hourly till 5.30 pm in winter and 7.30 pm in summer.

PLACES of INTEREST

Shepperton Studios, at nearby Littleton, have produced some world-famous films, including *Alien, Flash Gordon, Judge Dredd, Dr Strangelove*, and Kenneth Branagh's *Hamlet* and *A Midwinter's Tale*. The studios are not open to the general public but a walk around the perimeter fence is fascinating for film buffs.

❽   Ring the bell for the ferry. Pay the ferryman (60p adults, children and cycles 30p, at the time of writing). It takes you to the pier by the slipway at the end of, amazingly enough, Ferry Lane. It is good to help keep an old tradition alive, and the ride makes a very pleasant end to the walk. Go up Ferry Lane.

❾   At Chertsey Road, turn right and walk back to the village square.

SUNBURY

Length : 3³/₄ miles

<table>
<tr><td>

Getting there: Turn south from Staines Road East (A308) onto French Street and then right at the T junction onto Thames Street. Railtrack: Sunbury, then bus 237.

</td><td>

Parking: There are three car parks around the periphery of Sunbury Park. From the car parks off The Avenue and Thames Street the walk may be picked up at point 5 (the walled garden), and from the

</td><td>

car park off Green Street at point 4.

Map: OS Pathfinder 1190 Weybridge, Esher & Hampton Court (GR 106685).

</td></tr>
</table>

Sunbury is an attractive Thames-side village with some fine Georgian houses, a pleasant riverside path which passes three small islands in the Thames, and Sunbury Park which consists of sweeping meadowland, tree-fringed paths and an unusual walled garden.

The walk begins at St Mary's parish church from where you go along Thames Street with its fine houses. You then walk along the more rural Halliford Road and take a pleasant partly tree-shaded path which passes riding paddocks, a cemetery and some attractive traditional cottages. After exploring Sunbury Park and its walled garden you return to the church

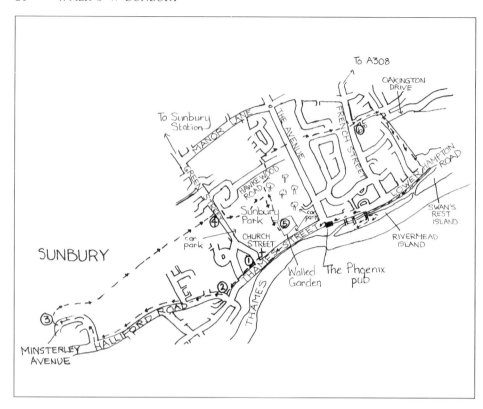

along footpaths, quiet residential streets, and a river path from where you can make a detour to one of the islands.

FOOD and DRINK

The Phoenix is a popular pub in an attractive old section of Thames Street, with good views of the river from its rear garden. The menu features main courses of pies and other pub favourites, and snacks, sandwiches and ploughman's lunches are also available. Two atmospheric bars at the front and one at the back serve Courage Directors and Courage Best. Children are welcome in the garden and rear bar, and dogs are welcome in the garden. Telephone: 01932 785358.

THE WALK

❶   Start at St Mary's parish church on the corner of Thames Street and Church Street. Walk south-west along Thames Street, pass the Flower Pot pub on the right, cross over Green Street and continue ahead.

❷   Turn right onto Halliford Road, pass Montford Road, Green Way and Vicarage Farm, continue ahead and turn right into Minsterley Avenue. Follow the avenue around till you come to the end of the houses on the right, where the road veers left.

❸   Turn right at the end of these houses

The walled garden at Sunbury Park.

and walk over the green. Turn right onto the tarmac road, called The Crofts, pass Freeman Close on the left, and when the road veers left, continue straight ahead along a public footpath. Pass a golf course on the left and, after crossing a stile, pass some riding paddocks on the right. Trees, which are a habitat for a variety of songbirds, now flank the path as you pass Sunbury Cemetery on the right. At the end of the cemetery continue ahead along the metalled track called School Walk. Pass some allotments and then some traditional cottages with well-kept front gardens, on the right. Continue ahead to Green Street and cross over the road.

❹ Turn right and enter Sunbury Park through the opening in the brick wall on the left, just before the Admiral pub on the right. Take the path straight ahead and at the fork bear left onto an indistinct path. Turn left at the T junction and at the fork, just before a steep dip, turn right, and walk along an indistinct path across the grass. Keep going straight ahead, passing three oak trees on the left. At the ha-ha on the right, and the beginning of the walled garden on the left, keep going straight ahead and enter the garden on its west side, by the gate on the left.

❺ After looking around the garden leave by the gate you entered. Turn right, pass the ha-ha and continue straight on to turn right onto a path following the far side of

---

PLACES of INTEREST

The **walled garden**, which consists of various styles of traditional garden, gives pleasure to both ocular and olfactory senses. The rose bed near the northern gate is planted with modern varieties and the one near the southern gate with those popular in Victorian times; many in the latter are strongly perfumed. The geometrical flowerbeds in the centre are parterres, a favourite feature in the gardens of 17th-century France. They surround a lion statue, a replica of one erected in 1895, which stood near the river opposite St Mary's church; the legend on a stone on the statue explains its origin. The portico around the northern gate came from Benwall House, which was in Green Street and was demolished in 1984. The garden is open from 7.45 am to 4.30 pm in winter, and to 8 pm in summer. Entrance is free.

---

the park. Leave the park by a footpath near the right corner. Cross Hawkewood Road and continue on the path to a grassy track as wide as a road. Turn right onto it and follow it over The Avenue to French Street.

❻   Cross straight over into Oakington Drive. Pass Ilex Close on the right and walk ahead across the green. At the end of the brick wall on the right, take the footpath to the right, signposted 'Lower Hampton Road'. Continue straight ahead at the end of the path, to Lower Hampton Road.

❼   Turn right here and continue in the same direction, along the path between the road and the river, passing Swan's Rest Island. Continue ahead and soon you will see the footbridge on the left to Rivermead Island. If you wish you can cross it to walk around the island's periphery. At the end of the riverside path continue ahead along Thames Street. There are many interesting traditional houses along this stretch of road. The Phoenix pub is on the left, opposite the end of The Avenue. Opposite the car park, take the crazy-paved path between the river and the road. Continue in the same direction to the church at the beginning of the walk.

NORWOOD

Length : 3 miles

Getting there: At Southall, leave The Broadway (A4020) on South Road (A3005) and follow this main road over the railway and canal to Norwood Green. Underground: Osterley (to join at point 4). Railtrack: Southall. The starting point is 1¹/₄ miles from Southall station; buses 120 and 232 go to Norwood Green from the station.

Parking: You may find on-street parking near the green.

Osterley House has a pay car park (free to National Trust members).

Maps: Street atlas, or OS Pathfinder 1174 Staines, Heathrow Airport & Richmond (GR 135786).

Norwood has managed to keep an exceptionally large village green, a great triangle to the north of the M4, just right for local fetes. Next to it is the traditional partnership of pub and church, and some of the village's remaining older buildings. The old village Free School, built in 1776, is past the pub, on the opposite side, and the Plough is a timber-framed 17th-century inn. Vine Cottage is an attractive building opposite St Mary's church; it has parts dating back to the 12th century, but much added-to and altered over the centuries (especially the 19th, almost inevitably).

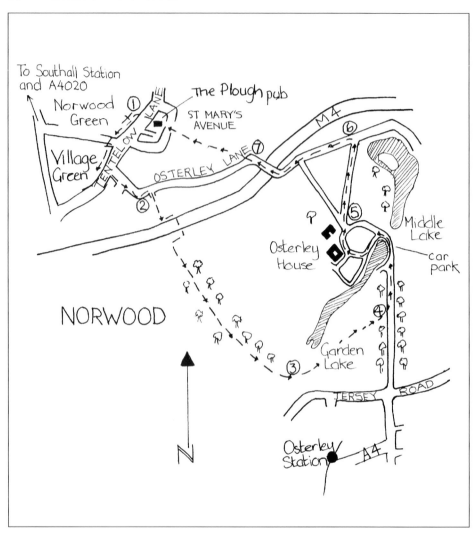

Bell-ringers are attracted to the set of bells in the Victorian tower. Nearer to the green is Norwood Hall, originally built between 1801 and 1803 by the renowned John Soane (architect of Pitshanger Manor in Ealing), but his design has been obscured by the demands of the building's present use as part of Ealing Tertiary College.

From the green, the walk crosses the M4 by a footbridge, which incidentally gives you a good view over the surrounding countryside. You then continue through a rural landscape on a tree-lined path between open fields, and then through the grounds of one of the treasures of the National Trust: Osterley House. After exploring the gardens, parkland and, perhaps, the house, you follow a country lane and footpath across a field back to the village centre.

THE WALK

❶ From the church, walk towards the green, pass Norwood Hall, cross onto the green and, just over halfway along, turn left onto Osterley Lane.

❷ Just after the sharp bend in the lane, turn right onto an unsignposted public footpath at the edge of the field (by the metal gate and stakes). Head along the trodden path towards the motorway, then turn left and cross the M4 by the footbridge. Follow the obvious path away from the motorway at the left edge of the field. Continue past an opening to the right between two lines of trees, initially, then

---

PLACES of INTEREST

The interior of **Osterley House** is worth seeing, as well as the exterior. Like Syon House, it is a monument to the work of Robert Adam. At Osterley he took an existing house and transformed the exterior by adding the great row of Ionic columns at the front, to enclose a courtyard, and remodelled most of the inside, building staircases and even designing beds and furniture. If you have had too much culture, there is a good tearoom in the old stable block. The house is open from the end of March to the end of October, Wednesday to Sunday and Bank Holiday Mondays; the grounds are open all year round. Telephone: 0181 560 3918.

---

follow the trees on your left to the end of the paddocks.

❸ Turn half left to follow a footpath at

St Mary's church.

the right of a field, running along a brick wall. Follow a sign to Wyke Green and enter the National Trust land, following the path between two fences, and go through the kissing gate.

❹   Turn left onto the avenue leading to the house. Go through the car park, skirt the edge of the lake and walk up to the house, and the adjacent stable block (housing the gift shop, tearoom and toilets).

❺   To return to Norwood, go through the vehicle gate, then, ignoring an avenue on your left, go straight down a track that becomes an avenue, leaving the estate at Jubilee Lodge.

❻   Turn left onto the bridleway, and continue on it as it becomes the metalled road, Osterley Lane. Follow this over the motorway. Just across the bridge, as the lane swings left, there is a track on the right

---

FOOD and DRINK

The Plough on Tentelow Lane, opposite the church, is a pub with a great, and genuine, ancient atmosphere: black wooden beams, brown ceilings and bare wooden and stone floors. At the rear is a safe enclosed garden with an extensive children's play area, as well as benches and tables (some under a spreading chestnut tree) for the adults. It's a Fuller's pub, so London Pride, ESB and Chiswick Bitter are on hand to wash down pub lunches such as pies, fish, omelettes or lighter fare such as excellent freshly prepared rolls and sandwiches. On some summer Sundays there is a barbecue. Telephone: 0181 574 1945.

---

barred by a metal gate.

❼   Go down the steps to the left of the gate and walk along the path diagonally across the field. Follow it between the houses, across the road, then down the side of the pub garden to come out onto Tentelow Lane and finish by the church.

HANWELL

Length : 4¹/₂ miles

Getting there: Turn south from the A40 onto Argyle Road (B452), turn right at the roundabout onto Ruislip Road East (B455), then left onto Greenford Avenue. Railtrack: Hanwell.	**Parking:** Opposite the church. You would then start the walk at point 2.	**Maps:** Street atlas, or OS Pathfinder 1158 Hillingdon & Wembley (GR 148807).

The view of Hanwell church and the surrounding parkland near the Wharncliffe rail viaduct was supposedly greatly admired by Queen Victoria en route to Windsor. The church, which overlooks Hanwell green, was designed by George Gilbert Scott and completed in 1841. Next to it is Brent Lodge Park and a small zoo.

A church and hamlet existed here in the 12th century. However, it was after the opening of the Great Western Railway in 1836 that the population increased significantly. Hanwell expanded further with the opening of a School for Orphans and Destitute Children built in 1856–7, when more modest houses appeared to accom-

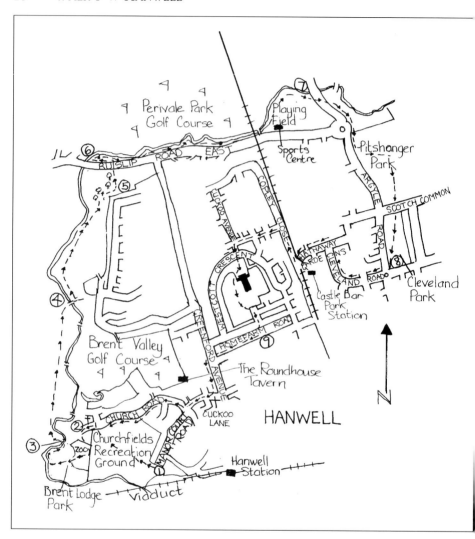

modate its employees. This imposing building once housed over a thousand pupils, one of whom was Charlie Chaplin. The building is now the Hanwell Community Centre.

This varied walk starts at Churchfields Recreation Ground, close to the viaduct. You continue to the church and enter Brent Lodge Park. After seeing the zoo you

continue along shady river paths, then through two pleasant parks and the grounds of the Hanwell Community Centre. You return to the church along Church Road.

THE WALK

❶ Begin at the south-east entrance to Churchfields Recreation Ground, on Manor

Hanwell Community Centre, once a Victorian institution.

Court Road. Enter the ground, turn right onto the tarmac path and continue ahead to Church Road and Hanwell church, passing a children's playground on the right.

❷   Facing the church, turn left into Brent Lodge Park and follow the tarmac path to the zoo. Take the tarmac path opposite the

---

FOOD and DRINK

The Roundhouse Tavern is a small friendly pub belonging to Brent Valley golf course. It opens at 8 am to serve breakfast to keen golfers – keen walkers can tuck in too. Children are welcome in the pleasant outdoor area. Food, available all day till 8 pm, includes sandwiches, mixed grills, Cajun chicken, omelettes and a range of desserts. Beers include Boddingtons and Fuller's London Pride. Telephone: 0181 566 3645.

---

entrance to the Animal Centre. At the end of the animal enclosure, walk ahead across the pitch 'n' putt course to the river Brent. Turn right and walk along the riverside path to wooden steps. Descend these and leave the park.

❸   Turn left, cross the footbridge and enter Brent River Park. Turn right onto the riverside path which has a Brent River Park Footpath sign. Keep on the path nearest the river and then, ignoring the footbridge on the right, go across Brent Valley golf course.

❹   At the far side turn right and cross the footbridge, then turn left onto the path along the right river bank. Veer left at the crosspaths to stay on the path nearest the river, and at the next crosspaths turn left.

PLACES of INTEREST

The small zoo in **Brent Lodge Park** is a delight for children. Outdoor enclosures (free) contain rabbits, guinea pigs and birds and an Animal Centre (small admission fee) houses a variety of small mammals. Opening times change but it is usually open during daylight hours. For further information contact Ealing's Countryside Service on 0181 758 5916.

Continue along the right river bank to wooden steps on the right. Ascend these, turn left at the top, and continue ahead, following the line of trees on the left. At the crosspaths turn right and continue ahead, still following a line of trees.

❺   At the end of the path turn left onto a tarmac path and walk to Ruislip Road. Cross over at the pelican crossing, turn left and walk along the road.

❻   Just before Greenford Bridge turn right onto a riverside footpath with a BRPW sign. Continue ahead and opposite the end of Greenford Avenue turn right and continue along the path as it skirts Ruislip Road. When the path ends, continue ahead on the pavement, still following the BRPW sign. Soon regain the path, go under the bridge, cross the tarmac drive and continue ahead. Ascend the wooden steps and continue ahead, passing a sports centre on the right. Stay near the river, still following the BRPW signs, and descend the wooden steps. Follow the line of trees around a playing field, then turn left onto a short footpath to Argyle Road.

❼   Turn right, following a BRPW sign, cross over the road and continue in the same direction. After passing the end of Ruislip Road East turn left onto a footpath signposted 'Perivale Lane'. Take the first turning right and continue ahead into Pitshanger Park. Continue ahead at the crossroads, and at the fork bear right. Continue ahead and ascend the steps to Scotch Common. Cross the road and enter Cleveland Park. Take the right fork and continue ahead to Cleveland Road.

❽   Turn right, cross over Argyle Road, and continue along Cleveland Road to the T junction. Turn left onto Hathaway Gardens and just before the roundabout, take the path ahead. Cross the footbridge over the line at Castle Bar Park station. Turn right onto Copley Close and then left onto Bordars Road. Turn left at Cuckoo Avenue and walk to the Hanwell Community Centre. At the entrance gate turn right and then left to enter the community centre grounds. Continue ahead on the path, passing the right side of the building and then ascending to a playing field. Turn left onto the path skirting the playing field. Leave by the kissing gate where the path veers right. Walk along Little John Road.

❾   Turn right onto Homefarm Road, and at the T junction left onto Greenford Avenue. Cross over, continue ahead and turn right onto Cuckoo Lane. Take the second turning right to reach the Roundhouse Tavern. To continue the walk, veer right onto Church Road and continue ahead to the north-west side of Churchfields Recreation Ground.

To return to Hanwell station, retrace your steps across the recreation ground to Manor Court Road.

EALING GREEN

Length : 2¹/₄ miles

Getting there: From the A4, go directly up Ealing Road (B455) past South Ealing station to St Mary's Square. Underground: South Ealing, Ealing Broadway, Ealing Common.

Parking: Car parks are available at the busy Broadway shopping centre. Try on-street parking between the parks and common, or use public transport.

Maps: Street atlas, or OS Pathfinder 1174 Staines, Heathrow Airport & Richmond (small part) and 1158 Hillingdon & Wembley (GR 177798).

If your knowledge of Ealing is restricted to the Broadway, the areas south of the Broadway are a pleasant surprise. You will find much less traffic, some remnants of fine buildings and green open spaces. Ealing was already quite a substantial settlement before the railways turned it into a fashionable Victorian suburb. Spen-cer Perceval, the only British Prime Minister to be assassinated, lived in Elm Grove in Ealing. Pitshanger Manor, owned by the borough and open as a museum, was built by John Soane for himself.

The walk starts in South Ealing, which still has the feel of a village in the area around St Mary's Square, a pleasant little

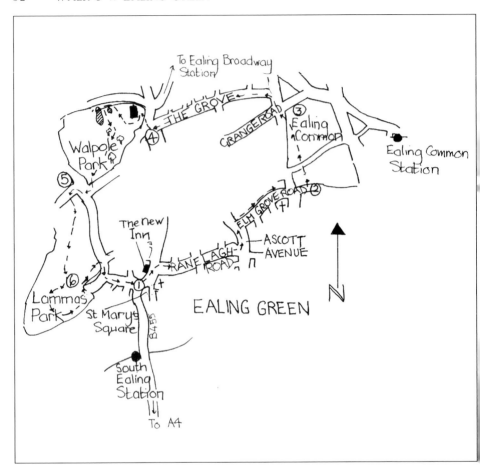

green lined by a Georgian terrace and a former Victorian fire station. St Mary's church itself is 18th century (on a much older site), extensively reworked in the 19th, which gave it the massive tower and Byzantine appearance. Quiet avenues, some lined with plane trees, lead you to Ealing Common. You follow more avenues to Walpole Park, and return to the start via Lammas Park.

THE WALK

❶ Starting opposite St Mary's Square,

walk towards St Mary's church. Its distinctive tower is quite a landmark. Follow St Mary's Road round to the left to another 'village green' centre, with a number of Georgian-style buildings. Explore St Mary's Place, a peaceful alley just beyond the New Inn, then cross St Mary's Road to go down Ranelagh Road opposite. Turn left into Ascott Avenue and take the first right into Elm Grove Road. At the end, pass All Saints' church, built in 1903 as a memorial to Spencer Perceval near the site of his home, Elm Grove.

View of the village green from Pitshanger Manor.

❷ Cross into Elm Avenue and walk onto Ealing Common. Follow the diagonal tarmac path a short way, then head over the grass roughly north. Sections of this part of the common have been left unmown, apparently to encourage wildlife. Cross the chestnut-lined avenue and continue parallel to the road on the left.

❸ At the next road crossing the common, leave it and take the second left, The Grove (not the first, Grange Road). Walk along this pleasant, leafy street, passing the King's Arms pub, then St Saviours Clergy House, noteworthy buildings as you approach Ealing Green.

❹ Cross the road and walk to the right over the green among the trees towards the entrance to Pitshanger Manor. Go through

---

FOOD and DRINK

The New Inn is an 18th-century coaching inn, with a surprisingly large rear garden, at the South Ealing end of St Mary's Road. Its impressive array of handpumps serve Theakston XB and Best, Abbot, John Smith's, Gillespie's Stout and a range of guest beers. A number of specialist Belgian beers are available in their correct glasses, rare attention to detail. Good food is on offer every day; check out the board for the specials. Pies with a flaky crust are a house speciality, and you can get a complete three-course meal or just a snack. This is a very pleasant, friendly pub. Telephone: 0181 840 4179.

PLACES of INTEREST

Pitshanger Manor, surrounded by Walpole Park, was built as his own house by the famous architect Sir John Soane in 1800–3, incorporating one wing of an earlier house. Soane was painstaking about interior design, and the house has been lovingly restored by the Borough of Ealing as a museum. After Soane sold the house it was acquired by Spencer Walpole for his sisters-in-law, the daughters of the assassinated Spencer Perceval, who had moved out of their home near Ealing Common. After the last surviving sister died in 1900, the house was sold to Ealing Council. The ground, with some fine trees, became Walpole Park, parts of which are often used for local events as a 'village green'. As with many borough museums, admission is free. Telephone: 0181 567 1227.

---

the war memorial gate, pass the left of the Manor, then go half right across the neat lawn and turn left at the perimeter path. Pass a low wall on the left bounding a small pond, then turn left. At the small aviary and shelter, turn half right to follow the avenue of chestnuts and oaks. Leave the park by Lammas Park Gate at the corner.

❺   Turn right onto Lammas Park Gardens, right again at the end onto Culmington Road, then immediately left onto Ellers Road and turn left into Lammas Park. There are tarmac paths following the park boundaries. Ignore them. Strike out diagonally over the grass. This is a typical 'English garden' type of parkland, with rolling grassland and fine trees. The tradition of tree-planting is now kept up by planting trees as memorials. Some of the younger trees have plaques at their base. Pass some sycamores and cross a chestnut avenue to reach the hedge by the bowling greens.

❻   Turn right and follow the hedge round the greens, turning left at the end and left again onto a tarmac path. Follow this path round to the left towards the park gates, passing a small memorial on the left of trees commemorating Scouts who fell in the two World Wars. Turn right out of the gate, right onto Church Lane and follow this round as it meets St Mary's Road at the square.

WALK 7
HAREFIELD
Length : 6 miles

| **Getting there:** Leave the A40 at Uxbridge Circus onto the B467 north, then turn left at the roundabout, onto Harvil Road. Underground: Northwood, then bus 331. | **Parking:** There is a small car park at Springwell Lock, reached from the A412 from Rickmansworth. You would then start the walk here, picking up the directions in point 6. | **Map:** OS Pathfinder 1139 Watford & Rickmansworth (GR 053906). |

Until the end of the 18th century Harefield was deeply rural, consisting of farms and country estates. One of the few surviving 17th-century buildings is the timber-framed King's Arms pub opposite the huge village green. The village development began with the opening of the Grand Union Canal in 1794 which linked London with Birmingham. The Harefield stretch of the canal runs alongside the river Colne. Lime kilns and flour and copper mills opened up along its towpath resulting in increased building to accommodate workers. These industries have long been abandoned and this pretty, rural stretch of canal is now popular with fishers and

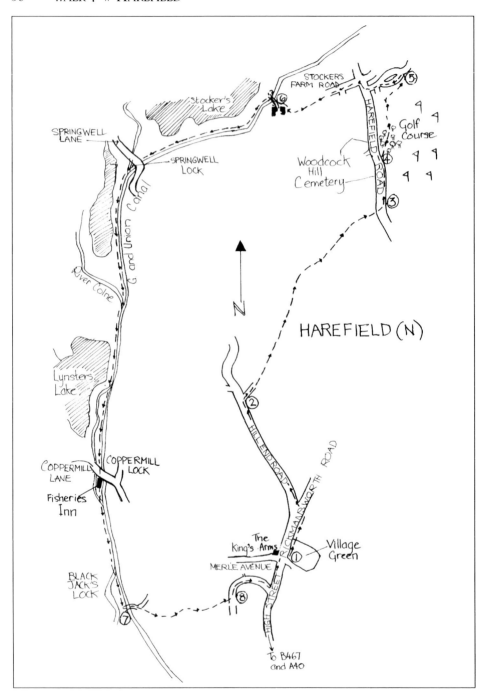

longboat owners, as well as walkers.

From the green you walk along the busy but pleasant Rickmansworth Road and then quieter Hill End Road, passing Harefield Hospital. You then take a path across fields to another fairly quiet rural road. You continue along a woodland path to a quiet road leading to the Grand Union Canal. After following the canal towpath, passing close to the river Colne and some artificial lakes, you return to Harefield.

THE WALK

❶ From the corner of the green, opposite the King's Arms, walk along Rickmansworth Road. At the fork bear left onto Hill End Road, passing the Harefield Hospital on the left.

❷ Just past the Child Link Learning Centre on the right, and Harefield Nursing Home on the left, turn right onto the tarmac drive signposted 'Public Footpath and Hillingdon Trail Northern Link'. At the end of the tarmac cross the stile on the right and go across the field, keeping right

---

FOOD and DRINK

Pub settings do not come much better than that of the Fisheries Inn, standing between the canal and the river Colne at Coppermill Lock. It has a spacious bar, a restaurant and a riverside garden. The extensive menu includes fish, vegetarian and steak dishes and a good choice of starters and desserts. Beers served are Tetley Bitter, Benskins, Calders Queen Ale, Guinness and one guest ale and Addlestones cask-conditioned cider is available. Children of all ages are welcome in the restaurant and garden, but under 14s are not allowed in the bar. Telephone: 01895 825623.

---

of the first tree in the middle of the field and left of the second. Cross another stile and continue ahead, still following the HTNL sign and keeping near the shrubbery on the left. At the end of the field cross the stile signposted for the HTNL and continue ahead. At the bottom of this field cross another stile on the left, signposted as a public footpath and the HTNL. Cross a footbridge and continue ahead between maize fields. When the fields are ploughed veer slightly right after the footbridge, to walk along the left edge of the field on the right. At the end of the path cross another stile and continue ahead, keeping near to the trees on the left. At the end of this path continue ahead along a drive.

❸ At the T junction with Harefield Road, turn left and continue ahead, taking care as there is no roadside verge on the first stretch of road. Just before the entrance to Woodcock Hill Cemetery on the left, turn right onto a footpath.

❹ Stay on this path as it veers left, cross a stile into woodland and veer left onto the uphill path. Keep on the main path, cross a stile and continue ahead, passing a golf course on the right. Keep ahead along a cinder track and at the end of it veer left, still at the edge of the golf course. Where the path veers right, cross the stile on the left. Keep on this path to Sherfield Avenue.

❺ Turn left and follow the road around to the T junction. Turn right, cross over and turn left onto Stockers Farm Road. At the end of the road continue ahead along the drive. At the farm buildings veer right to walk to the right of them.

❻   Turn right, cross over the bridge and climb over the metal barrier on the right to reach the Grand Union Canal towpath. Turn right, go under the bridge, and continue along the towpath. Go under the next bridge at Springwell Lock and Arm and continue along the towpath, passing Springwell Reed Bed Nature Reserve, an important waterfowl habitat, on the right. Cross the bridge over the Colne, where longboats are moored in the adjacent Maplecross Basin. Continuing ahead along the towpath, you will soon get glimpses of Lynsters Lake, a flooded gravel pit, on the right. You approach Coppermill Lock and the Fisheries Inn past some impressive brick mill buildings, originally paper mills but converted into copper mills at the end of the 18th century. Some have recently been renovated. A sluice enables canoeists to practise whitewater slaloming – a rare sight on a canal. Continue along the towpath.

❼   At Black Jack's Lock you leave the towpath and cross the bridge over the canal. Turn right and, where the road turns left, cross the stile straight ahead to a field. Cross the field, veering left. Where the line of

---

PLACES of INTEREST

Stocker's Lake, near point 6 of the walk, is a flooded gravel pit which is now a nature reserve and a habitat for a great variety of waterfowl. It is managed by the Herts & Middlesex Wildlife Trust. To visit the reserve you need to apply in advance for a free entry permit, become a member of the Trust, or become a Friend of Stocker's Lake, to support their work. The Trust is based in St Albans, and can be contacted on 01727 858901.

---

trees at the far side of the field protrudes slightly, cross a stile, and take the path ahead and uphill through woodland and signposted 'Hillingdon Trail'. When the path levels out continue ahead. Follow the path as it skirts the left side of a field. At the end of the field veer slightly left and cross a stile. Ignore the stile and path on the right, signposted 'Hillingdon Trail'. Cross the stile at the other side of the field and continue ahead to Merle Avenue.

❽   Turn left here and follow the road around to the High Street. Turn left and continue ahead to return to the green.

SOUTH HAREFIELD

Length : 5¹/₂ miles

Getting there: Leave the A40 at Uxbridge Circus onto the B467 north, then turn left at the roundabout, onto Harvil Road. Underground: Uxbridge, then bus 331. Railtrack: Denham.	Parking: At the Moorhall Road entrance to the Denham Quarry area. You would then start the walk at point 7.	Maps: OS Pathfinder 1158 Hillingdon & Wembley (and a short section on 1139 Watford & Rickmansworth) (GR 053896).

South of the main village of Harefield, Church Hill has been another centre for settlement for centuries. The White Horse pub has been an inn since 1625, the Countess of Derby's Almshouses just down the hill from the pub date from a few years later, and there used to be a 14th-century manor house further down, to the east of the church. St Mary's church itself, set back from the road, is the main feature of this area, a happy mix of building styles from Norman through 14th-century to 19th-century restorations, the walls inside and out covered in monuments.

Harefield boasts some of the finest scenery in Middlesex, and this walk gives

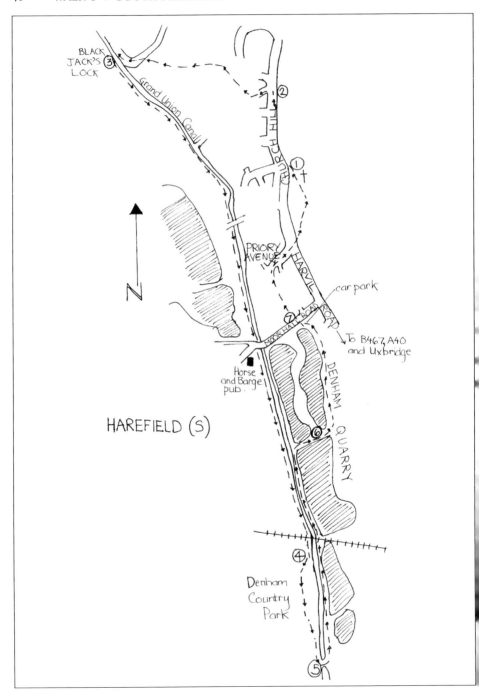

St Mary's church.

you a stunning view over rolling fields, the river Colne, Grand Union Canal and gravel pit lakes, and then leads you alongside these countryside waterways. You will have many opportunities to see waterfowl, and also some natural woodland in Denham Country Park. You return to Harefield through Denham Quarry, parkland now owned by Hillingdon Council and the site of more lakes resulting from the extraction of gravel.

THE WALK

❶ From the church, go up the lane to Church Hill, climbing past the almshouses on the right, and the White Horse on the left.

❷ Turn left onto Bird Lane, the unmetalled track signposted as the Hillingdon Trail. Go straight across the next road down the footpath, then cross a stile, keep to the

---

FOOD and DRINK

The White Horse pub is just up from the almshouses on Church Hill. One of a number of excellent pubs in Harefield, it has been a pub for over 350 years. It serves Thomas Greenall's Original, Tetley Bitter, Adnams and Shipstone's beers, with a different guest beer every week or two. Food is very much a feature, and is served at lunchtimes and evenings seven days a week. Light snacks to three-course meals are available from a fixed menu, and as many as eight daily specials are chalked up on the board. Telephone: 01895 822144.

Widewater Lock.

footpath and cross the next stile into a field. Turn left at the end of the field, following Hillingdon Trail signs. You have a very fine view from here down over the Colne valley. Cross the next stile and go down diagonally through the next field, leaving it at the stile near the canal. Walk along the road parallel to the canal, then follow it round to the left, crossing the canal by Black Jack's Lock. Turn right onto the towpath.

❸   Go under the bridge; now follow a long section of towpath south, passing under a disused bridge, then Moorhall Road bridge just before the Horse and Barge canalside pub. A milepost shows that Braunston is 79 miles along the canal to the north. Pass by a large marina on the left and lakes on your

right. Go under the railway viaduct and, very shortly after, note the pond and reed beds on the right, part of Denham Country Park. The entrance to this is on your right, just after a small weir on your right taking off water from the canal. You can now either walk through this nature reserve, which includes wooded areas, by turning right and following the directions in point 4, or keep to the towpath until the next footbridge, then follow directions from point 5.

❹   Go down the steps and follow the path; turn left onto the bridleway – do not go through the kissing gate. You are walking past Flagmoor Coppice and Covert on your left and Flagmoor Pasture on your right.

Beyond the pasture is the river Colne – the woods and meadows are on an island between the two waterways. Cross a bridge of wooden sleepers and pass a line of chestnuts, then turn left onto the footpath signposted 'Denham Quarry' to come back to the canal by the footbridge.

❺   Cross the canal, follow the path away from it, between wooden railings, then turn left onto a track entering Denham Quarry, which runs next to a gravel pit lake on the right. The lake is a conservation site and hosts a range of waterfowl. You might catch a glimpse of a kingfisher; cormorants and herons also compete with the human anglers. Keep your dog away from the water – the lake has toxic algae in it. At the end of the lake, follow the tarmac path to the left under the railway viaduct. Go all the way past another lake on your right, then follow the path to the right.

❻   You are now passing the marina seen earlier from the other side of the canal. At the end of the marina, go straight on along the gravel path, following Colne Valley Trail markers. Follow the gravel path round to the left, then go through the fence onto the road. Pass a metal gate, then turn left onto the gravel path, following more Trail markers. Walk through wooded parkland and a picnic area. Leave Denham Quarry through another wooden barrier and walk through the car park to the road.

❼   Cross Moorhall Road carefully and take the footpath opposite on the left of the grass. Pass tennis courts and the community centre and turn right at the road. Follow Priory Avenue to the main Harvil Road, cross it, and take the track opposite, just to the right of the bus stop. Follow this track round to the left to the church.

RUISLIP

Length : 2³/₄ miles

Getting there: Leave the A40 at Hillingdon Circus, taking the B466 north through Ickenham to Ruislip High Street. Underground: Ruislip.	**Parking:** At the Manor Farm site near the library.	**Map:** OS Pathfinder 1158 Hillingdon & Wembley (GR 092876).

The old centre of Ruislip village, just off the busy main road, makes an astonishingly peaceful contrast to the bustle of the High Street. There is still a village atmosphere to the area around the parish church and the Manor Farm Complex, a group of mediaeval barns which is a real community resource, incorporating the local library, open space for a pond and bowling green and Manor Farm House.

The walk starts by St Martin's church which dates back to the 13th century, and has been reworked since by many hands including those of George Gilbert Scott. I is shielded from the traffic by a timber framed house on the north and by a row o low timber-framed buildings on the High Street side. The walk passes through the

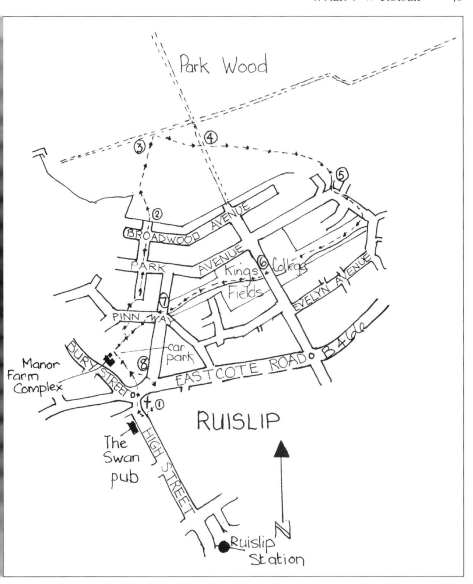

barn complex, into Park Wood, part of the ancient Middlesex woodland, mainly oak and ash, with stands of silver birch. You return via open meadows, King's College Fields, which are very popular with local dog-walkers.

THE WALK

❶ Start on the north side of the church, facing the group of cottages. Take the path to the left through the lychgate in the short passageway between buildings, to emerge on the High Street, opposite the Swan.

Park Wood.

Turn right and go to the corner, at the roundabout. Cross the road, carefully, and, just to the left of the war memorial, go down the public footpath to the library and Manor Farm Complex. On the right, opposite the barns, are the remains of a motte and bailey castle. Follow the tarmac track round to the right through the white gates to Manor Farm House, then walk down through the parkland, keeping to the left side. Turn right at the concrete road, follow it a short way, then take a footpath half left across the lawn towards the white stone bridge. Cross Pinn Way, do not enter Mead Way, but go into the green area by the bridge, following the obvious footpath. Go left at the first fork to the end of the cul-de-sac, and walk up Sherwood Avenue, crossing two roads to enter Park Wood.

❷   Take the right fork at the end of the wooden fences, and the path bears left. Turn right onto a broader path joining from the left, and follow this alternately stony and muddy path to a point just *before* a

---

FOOD and DRINK

The Swan on High Street, opposite the church, is an old coaching inn. Nowadays it is a popular Taylor Walker pub, serving Burton and Tetley bitters and Old Speckled Hen. In good weather, there are outside tables on the broad pavement that give a good view of the old part of the village. Hot daily specials, vegetarian meals, cold platters and filled baguettes are chalked up on the board. Telephone: 01895 622248.

The preserved pump in High Street, with St Martin's tower in the background.

junction with a main track wide enough for vehicles.

❸   Turn right onto a path heading roughly south-east. Silver birches are now predominant. Cross two plank bridges over ditches. At another main vehicle-width track, a modest short cut is possible: turn right onto it and head straight down out of the woods and along King's College Road, crossing two roads until you reach the playing field entrance on the right, and continue from point 6. Otherwise, go on to point 4.

❹   Go straight over the broad track onto an obvious path opposite, passing a short post numbered '8' (on the back). At the entrance to a clearing is a sturdy stile, completely redundant as there is no fence, near another post. In the clearing, turn half right onto a fairly clear grassy path passing right of an isolated tree back into the woods. The track veers left, then turn right at a junction and follow the path out of the woods.

❺   Turn left onto Elmbridge Drive, go past the end of River Close on the right and the remaining houses, then turn half right onto the green open space and walk to the trees lining the river Pinn, following them through two meadows on your right to reach King's College Road. Turn right onto the road and follow the left side to a public footpath sign pointing through a gateway into playing fields.

❻   Go through the gateway, turn left to pass a dilapidated pavilion, then turn right and walk diagonally across the running track and leave the field at the corner by

> **PLACES of INTEREST**
>
> The site of **Manor Farm** was granted to the Norman knight Ernulf de Hesdin, shortly after the Conquest. He held a motte and bailey castle here; the ruins can still be seen. He passed the site on to the Benedictine Abbey of Bec. It was confiscated, not by Henry VIII for once, but by Henry V, as an alien property shortly before Agincourt. It was passed to King's College, Cambridge, in 1451. When the College sold Park Wood to Middlesex County Council in 1932, Manor Farm was included as a gift to the people of Ruislip. The 16th-century Little Barn houses the public library, and can thus be seen during opening hours. Local events and exhibitions regularly take place in the adjacent Great Barn (1280–1300), providing an opportunity to see its preserved interior. Check times with Manor Farm Library: 01895 633651.

the river. Go straight on into the large open meadow and walk alongside the river Pinn, here a pleasant 8 foot wide stream.

❼   Leave the meadow by the gate to cross the next road, turn left, cross the river, then walk across the grass on your right by the river. Look across to the left when the houses end for a break in the hedge. Leave through it, cross Pinn Way, enter the grassland opposite and turn right. Walk half left over the grass to regain the concrete road used (in the other direction) in point 1. Turn left and retrace your steps through the parkland, past the Manor Farm House and barn complex.

❽   At the end of the drive, turn left to pass the war memorial and turn right to view the half-timbered building opposite. Cross the road and enter the churchyard by the lychgate on your left to finish.

PINNER

Length : 4 miles

<table>
<tr><td>Getting there: Pinner High Street is just off the A404. If you wish to begin the walk at Harrow Museum, turn off the A404 at Station Road, and continue along Parkside Way. Underground: Pinner.</td><td>Parking: There is a long-stay pay car park by the station, part of the Sainsbury's complex. Alternatively, there is a free car park at Harrow Museum and Heritage Centre.</td><td>Maps: Street atlas, or OS Pathfinder 1158 Hillingdon & Wembley (GR 124897).</td></tr>
</table>

Pinner's High Street, with its 16th-century half-timbered buildings and 18th-century brick buildings, looks exactly like a rural village street from a film set. It is overlooked by St John's parish church, parts of which are 14th century.

Pinner developed after the Metropolitan Railway reached it in 1886. However, most development was in keeping with its traditional buildings, a number of which survive. One of the finest is Pinner House. From 1788 to 1811 it was the home of the Reverend Walter Williams, vicar of Pinner and Harrow, whose wife Mary Beauderic was the granddaughter of Charles II and Nell Gwynn.

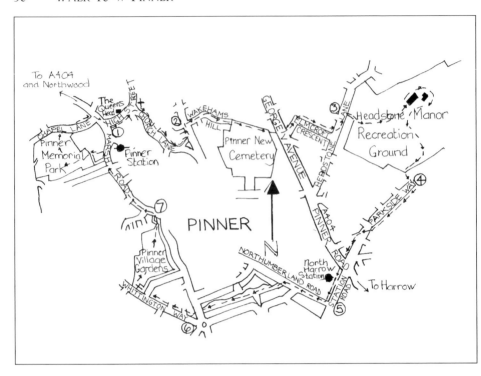

This varied walk starts at the High Street, continues to St John's church and then to Pinner House. Some fairly quiet, pleasant roads take you to Headstone Manor Recreation Ground and the Harrow Museum and Heritage Centre, where a

---

FOOD and DRINK

The Queens Head pub, one of Pinner's oldest inns, was built in the 16th century. It was originally called the Crown and was renamed the Queens Head in the 18th century. It has a large lounge with genuinely old beams, dark wood benches and tables and wood panelled walls. The menu includes steak, scampi, steak and ale pie and vegetable bake as well as daily specials. Beers served are Benskins Best Bitter and Burton and Young's ales. Telephone: 0181 868 9844.

---

rare sight awaits you – a 14th-century moated manor house. The return is through three delightful and contrasting parks. In the first you walk by the Yeading Brook; in Pinner Village Gardens you walk across grassland dotted with a variety of trees; and in Pinner Memorial Park you wend your way between tall pine trees.

THE WALK

❶ Walk uphill along the High Street, turn right onto Church Lane, cross over the road and go through the lychgate into St John's churchyard, where you can't miss the unusual 1809 Loudon memorial; the stone coffin shape above the arch is only ornamentation, there is a burial vault below. If the church is open, explore the interior; opposite the entrance, the 15th-

Open day at Pinner House.

century font has a modern elaborately carved wooden cover.

Leave by the lychgate, turn left, and walk along Church Lane, passing Pinner House on the left. At the green, where the road forks, veer left. The green's fountain, erected in 1886, is a memorial to William Arthur Tooke JP, who financed the restoration of St John's church in 1880. Continue ahead and at the T junction, turn left.

❷ Turn right, onto Wakehams Hill. Ignore the footpath on the left and at the end of the road take the tarmac path straight ahead. At the end of the path continue straight ahead to George V Avenue. Cross over the dual carriageway and go along Elmcroft Crescent. Follow the

road around as it turns right, and continue to the T junction. Turn left onto Headstone Lane, cross over and continue in the same direction.

❸ At the end of the houses on the right, turn right onto Headstone Manor Recreation Ground and walk ahead on the tree-fringed path. Just before the path veers right, turn left, and cross the sports field. At the tarmac path turn right and continue ahead to enter the Harrow Museum and Heritage Centre through the wide metal gate. After looking around leave by the same gate. Walk straight ahead and at the end of the children's playground turn left, staying on the tarmac path. Stay on this path as it veers right, then turns left and

---

PLACES of INTEREST

Pinner's oldest surviving house, **Headstone Manor**, is a 14th-century moated manor house in the Harrow Museum and Heritage Centre. Also here, is a giant 16th-century tithe barn and a smaller barn and granary. The land was originally a working farm owned by the Archbishops of Canterbury until it was 'acquired' by Henry VIII in 1545, to be passed on to a favourite. It is now owned by the Borough of Harrow. The barn holds a small museum, café and toilets. Admission is free and opening times are Wednesday to Friday 12.30 pm to 5 pm, Saturday, Sunday and bank holidays 10.30 am to 5 pm. Telephone: 0181 861 2626.

---

crosses a bridge over a stream. Continue ahead, passing allotments on the left.

❹ Leave the grounds and at the T junction turn right onto Parkside Way. Stay on this road as it veers right, then left, and becomes Station Road. At Pinner Road, a major crossroads, continue straight ahead towards the overhead railway bridge.

❺ After North Harrow station turn right onto Northumberland Road. Cross over,

and at the bridge over the Yeading Brook, turn left and enter the park through the gate. Continue ahead along the tarmac path to the left of the brook. At the crossroads keep straight ahead, leave the park, cross over the road and continue ahead on a track which soon veers left.

❻ At Whittington Way turn right and continue ahead to Pinner Village Gardens, on the right. Enter the gardens and walk straight ahead across the grass, then, after passing the clump of shrubbery on the left, veer left. Turn right onto the tarmac path and stay on this path to the far side of the park.

❼ Leave the park, turn left, and left again onto Marsh Road. Continue ahead and turn left into Pinner Memorial Park. Walk a little way along the tarmac path, then turn right and walk across the grass between the pine trees. At the tarmac path turn right and leave the park. Cross over the road and go under the railway bridge. Turn right and then left to regain the High Street.

WALK 11

HARROW

Length : 3¹/₂ miles

Getting there: From the A40, take the A4127 north from Greenford, then turn left onto Sudbury Hill to the village centre. Underground: Harrow on the Hill; South Kenton (near point 5).

Parking: This is very restricted on the hill; try near the recreation ground on Norval Road (and start the walk at point 5) or the shopping centre north of the Harrow on the Hill station (and start at point 3).

Maps: Street atlas, or OS Pathfinder 1158 Hillingdon & Wembley (GR 153875).

The centre of Harrow *is* the school, founded in 1572. It numbers Byron, Sheridan, King Hussein of Jordan, his ill-fated cousin Faisal II (the last King of Iraq) and Churchill amongst its alumni. Many of the pubs in Harrow boast that Churchill drank in them; World War II may have been won in the public houses of Harrow. The chapel was built by Sir George Gilbert Scott. Other prominent school buildings, and those of the associated 'service in-dustries', such as bookshops, outfitters' and tea rooms, give the centre a special flavour of its own.

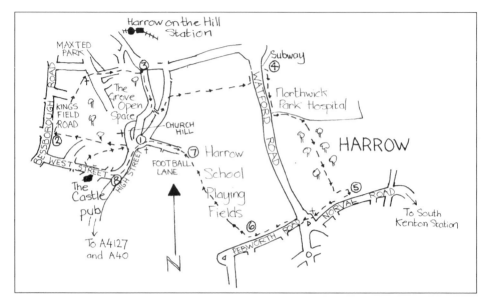

The walk starts near the only part of the school regularly open to the public, The Old Schools. Next is St Mary's church, whose spire on the hill is a landmark for miles. Byron spent hours here contemplating the view from the Peachey Stone, which is now surrounded by railings to deter imitators. You descend through the churchyard to some of the open spaces of Harrow, including the school farm and the playing fields, through which you return on your way back up the hill.

THE WALK

❶ Start at the foot of Church Hill, where it leaves High Street. Old Speech Room Gallery is on the left. Go up the hill through the lychgate into the churchyard. Pass the south porch, with its sad memorial to Byron's daughter Allegra at the bottom right. Continue on the tarmac path past the west end of the church; the Peachey Stone is to the left, just before you go down a set of steps through the churchyard into open parkland. Pass a row of poplars, then head right of the fence down to the road.

❷ Turn right onto the path at the edge of the parkland and follow it round past the school and church, crossing the road to take the path opposite to The Grove Open

The Old Schools building.

Space. Head across and down to go in front of the war memorial.

❸   At the junction with Grove Hill, turn right up the hill, by a copse. Take the first left, Davidson Lane, then turn left onto Peterborough Road. Just past The Garlands, turn right onto a signposted public footpath to Watford Road. At this busy main road, turn left to take the subway.

❹   Turn right out of the subway; take the road in front of the hospital buildings parallel to Watford Road. At a T junction, rejoin the Watford Road path, and after about 100 yards, turn left at the end of the hedge onto The Ducker Footpath, before the wooden fence. Follow the path through the wood, keeping the fence on your right, then emerge into open grass – actually a pitch 'n' putt course. Bear right at the edge of the grass, and keep to the right-hand side as the faint path meanders alongside a stream and shrubbery to your right, leading you into playing fields – again keep to the right. At the end of the field, turn left. There is a broad uncut verge which is a haven for plants and insects – watch the fence carefully, and turn right at the first exit, where the fence abruptly shifts back.

❺   Turn right onto Norval Road, and at its end cross the green triangle and the busy Watford Road. Turn right and then left into Pebworth Road. Just before Mulgrave Road, turn right onto a footpath to Harrow School Farm.

❻   Cross the stile, then head uphill across the field to the corner gate; head just to the right of the steeple on the hill. Go through

---

PLACES of INTEREST

The Old Schools on Church Hill contains the original school building of 1608, although the exterior, including grand windows overlooking the garden, is early 19th century. The building also contains the **Old Speech Room Gallery**, which holds public art exhibitions. Telephone: 0181 869 1205 for opening times. **The Cat Museum:** A room of impractical cats; antique cats as depicted in various media. Free admission, open Thursday, Friday and Saturday. 49 High Street, Harrow on the Hill. Check opening times on 0181 422 1892.

---

the kissing gate, along the path between the two fences, through another gate and then straight on. Cross the metal bars at the end of the next field and the bridge over the brook. Pass a redundant stile (there is no longer a fence) into Harrow School playing fields. Follow the right of way straight on between two pitches, then to the right of the next pitch, to arrive at the track near the public footpath signpost.

❼   Turn left here, then half right to go through the wooden gate uphill, following the sign to Peterborough Hill. Go up to the top of the lane, then turn left at the main road to come to the centre of Harrow. Go up the broad flight of stone steps, and turn round at the top to admire the school chapel, then go down Church Hill onto High Street.

❽   Turn right down West Street. Pass the Castle pub on the left and then, after the end of Victoria Terrace, turn right onto a public footpath leading round to the right and left onto the parkland below the church. Walk uphill back to the church to complete the walk.

NORTHOLT

Length : 7 miles

Getting there: From the A40, turn north onto the A312, then right down Church Road to reach the village centre. Underground: Northolt.	**Parking:** There is some space near the church and village green. The Crown has a car park for patrons.	**Maps:** Street atlas, or OS Pathfinder 1158 Hillingdon & Wembley (GR 132841).

Just off the busy A312 is a very peaceful, traditional village centre: a small but charming green next to a stream, with a pub on one side and the highly picturesque church, St Mary's, on the other. Before the war, Northolt was home to Northolt Park, a fashionable racecourse, where aristocrats and celebrities met – George Formby rode here in a real race. The site has been built over, but the churchyard appears to retain a racing connection – the grave of Edmund Tattersall, apparently the second head of the family firm of horse-breeders and auctioneers.

Starting at the village green, the walk leads you past the very pretty mediaeval St Mary's church standing proud on its hill, through the churchyard, down through

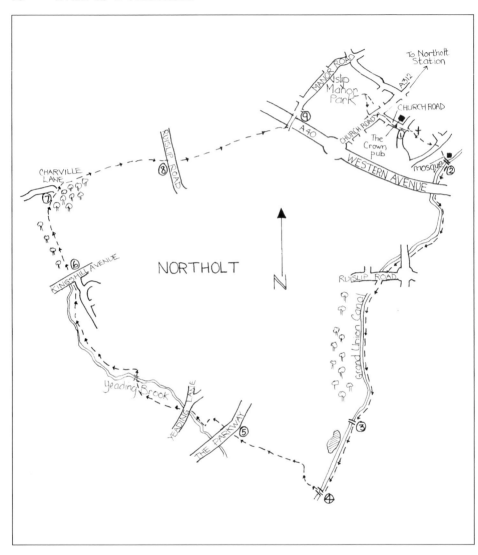

parkland, to pass a new mosque – at the time of writing, the largest in Europe. Then you follow the Grand Union Canal tow-path and continue through Yeading Brook Open Space, a line of meadows alongside the brook which include some of the finest natural habitat in West London. A country lane, rural paths, and finally a walk through

Islip Manor Park in the centre of Northolt bring you back to the start.

THE WALK

❶   From the green, walk up to the church and, at the south porch, turn right. Leaving the churchyard, turn left into Belvue Park and walk down its left side (with a good

The Grand Union Canal.

view of the new mosque) to leave it at the left corner. Cross Rowdell Road, to take a

footpath opposite, waymarked with a yellow arrow and dog rose. Pass the mosque complex on your left and cross the canal by the footbridge.

❷ Turn right down to the towpath, heading away from the mosque. Go under Western Avenue bridge, then under a succession of bridges and buildings that cross the canal. Cross the Ealing/Hillingdon boundary.

❸ Ignore a footbridge supported by a white concrete arch, keeping to the towpath. Pass a marina on the right. Re-enter Hillingdon, and pass a row of poplar trees by a playing field.

❹   Cross the canal by the footbridge, then turn half right off the tarmac onto a broad grass path. Follow this round to the right, ignoring a path to the left. Keep on the grass track. Ignore a Hillingdon Trail sign to the right, and veer left. Enter a meadow; stay on the right, by the hedge. Cross a tarmac path.

❺   Follow the path through the tunnel under the bypass, then, before the houses, turn left onto a grass track at the edge of the meadow. Veer left round the play area, then turn right at a signpost, to head through the next field towards the road. Keep the hedge (and brook) on your left. Go through the gate onto the road, turn left, follow the road across the brook, then turn right into the opening signposted 'Hillingdon Trail and Nature Reserve'. Walk straight through this to exit at the right corner. Turn right onto the footpath and cycleway, cross the bridge, then, immediately after, turn left into the meadow and continue on along the left side, passing a footbridge on the left and staying on the mown grass path. Leave the meadows by the brook and cross Kingshill Avenue.

❻   Enter the next part of Yeading Brook Meadows by the kissing gate opposite Attlee Road. Go through this nature reserve, keeping to a path at the right-hand side. Leave the field at the narrow end through the wood, following waymarks, and cross a plank bridge and stile onto the lane

❼   Turn right, go through the gate, then turn left onto a track and turn right onto a (possibly overgrown) path by fencing at the side of the building. Follow this track all the way along past woods and the shooting grounds on the right, with a view over fields to the airfield on the left. Pass the site of a (demolished) moated manor house and come out onto Ruislip Road.

❽   Cross the road, following the ramble sign opposite at the right-hand side of a meadow. Continue between two hedges and follow the public footpath across the golf course, between two hedges once you reach the tall fence. At the end of the golf course, turn left onto a tarmac path, then follow it to the right and cross the footbridge.

❾   Turn left into Islip Manor Road, then, opposite Arnold Road, turn right onto a waymarked footpath and go through Islip Manor Park. Pass the play area, turn left, then turn right near the building and follow the path out of the park. Cross over the main road and walk down Church Road opposite to return to the village green.

STANMORE

Length : 3³/₄ miles

Getting there: Take the A5 to the junction with London Road (A410) and turn westwards. Underground: Stanmore, then walk or take bus H12.

Parking: There is a car park off the north side of the Broadway between Dennis Lane and Stanmore Hill, another one off Elm Park, just south of Church Road, and a third one next to the Underground station.

Maps: Street atlas, or OS Pathfinder 1139 Watford & Rickmansworth (GR 167922).

Stanmore has a long history. The name derives from 'stoney mere' and, mere being an ancient word for pond, this presumably refers to the ponds at the top of Stanmore Hill, which were possibly dug to provide water for a Roman camp. Stanmore Common was reputedly the site of the last battle between Boadicea and the Romans. The village was a major posting station on Watling Street, the Roman road that once linked London to the north-west via Verulamium (present day St Albans). It was also a major centre of the pottery industry.

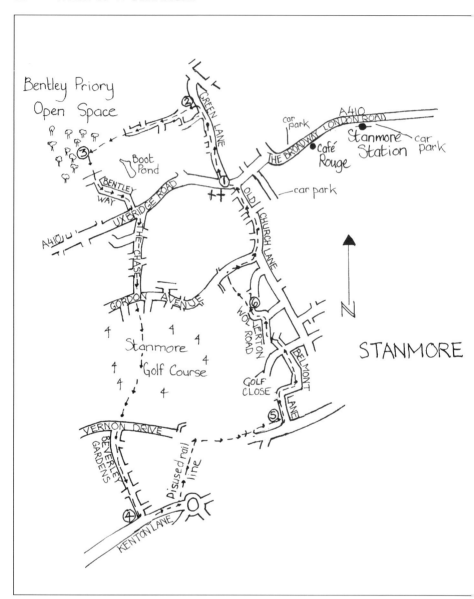

Two churches stand in the centre of the village. One, Great Stanmore old church, is now a picturesque ruin. It was built of red brick, made locally at brickworks which used to be on Old Redding. It was completed in 1632. The church was de scribed by Pevsner as one of the best ruins in Middlesex. Next to it is the new church, S John's, built in 1850. Near the churches are some fine timber-framed buildings.

Old Church Lane, Stanmore.

The walk begins at the churches, from where you walk along Green Lane which has some picturesque, traditional cottages. You briefly enter Bentley Priory Open Space and then proceed south to take a leafy path across Stanmore golf course.

FOOD and DRINK

The Café Rouge, 67–69 The Broadway, is one of the chain of these successful atmospheric restaurants. It serves well-prepared French-influenced meals and snacks. The fixed price three-course lunch and dinner menu is particularly good value. A wide range of lagers, wines and speciality coffees is available. The restaurant is between the end of Old Church Lane and Stanmore station. It is open from 10 am to 11 pm. Telephone: 0181 385 7273.

From the path's highest point there are splendid, panoramic views south to Harrow and beyond. After a short walk along streets you take a path along a disused railway track which has been reclaimed by nature and has a rich variety of shrubbery and wild flowers. You return via some quiet residential streets to Old Church Lane with its fine, apparently Tudor houses, which were actually built in the first half of this century.

THE WALK

❶ Begin at the two churches. After exploring the churchyard leave by the lychgate, cross over Church Road, and walk up Green Lane, passing picturesque Green Lane Cottages on the left.

❷   After the cottages turn left onto a tarmac drive signposted 'Park Cottages'. Continue straight ahead after these cottages, passing a school on the right. Continue to the end of Embry Way and take the footpath straight ahead, signposted 'Bentley Priory and Clamp Hill'. Go through the kissing gate and continue ahead. Cross over the tarmac path and continue ahead on the path signposted 'Clamp Hill' or, if you wish, turn left to make a short detour to Boot Pond.

❸   Just before the wood, turn left onto a footpath with high wooden fencing on both sides. Go through the gate and continue straight ahead along Bentley Way. Cross over Uxbridge Road and walk down The Chase. At the end of The Chase cross over Gordon Avenue and take the paving-stoned footpath ahead, signposted 'Vernon Drive'. Continue along this tree-shaded path flanked by Stanmore golf course. The path soon begins to ascend gradually and at its highest point there are fine views to the south. The path now descends and ends at Vernon Drive. Cross over and walk straight ahead along Beverley Gardens.

❹   Turn left onto Kenton Lane. Cross over the bridge and turn left to walk across a car park to the beginning of the path along a disused railway line. Follow this path to the end, then turn right onto a tarmac path and continue ahead through a housing estate. Ignore the right turn and continue ahead along a paving-stoned path. At the end continue ahead along Wemborough Road.

❺   Turn left onto Belmont Lane and

PLACES of INTEREST

This walk takes you through a small section of **Bentley Priory Open Space**, an extensive rural area consisting of a deer park, woodland and open meadows with fine views of London. If you wish to explore it further there are many signposted footpaths. The area is named after Bentley Priory which once stood in the northern section. The priory was founded around 1170 and suppressed in the Reformation, a house was built on its site in 1766, and enlarged by Sir John Soane in 1790. It became the property of the Air Ministry in 1925 and RAF Flight Command HQ. The Battle of Britain was controlled from here. There is no public admission to the house.

follow it around as it veers right and then left. Cross Golf Close and take the tarmac path ahead and to the right of the end of the houses. At the end turn right onto Wolverton Road and continue ahead along the road signposted to (among others) Omega Cottage and Alpha Cottage.

❻   Just beyond the path signposted 'Gordon Avenue', go through the gate on the left into a fenced-off area. Walk ahead and at the T junction turn right. Follow this path all the way through Montrose Walk and turn right onto Gordon Avenue. Cross over the road and continue ahead to the T junction with Old Church Lane. Turn left and continue ahead, passing the Manor House, the Almshouses, Church House and Conrad's Cottage on the right. Despite appearances, these are not genuine Tudor but were built in the 20th century for the occupant of the Manor House. The churches from where you started the walk are at the top of here, on the left.

ARKLEY

Length : 4³/₄ miles

Getting there: Turn westwards off Barnet Hill (A1000) just south of the High Street onto Wood Street (A411) which becomes Barnet Road. Underground:
Edgware or High Barnet, then bus 107.

Parking: There is a small car park behind St Peter's church.

Maps: Street atlas, or OS Pathfinder 1140 Barnet & Enfield (GR 219954).

Arkley developed after the opening of East Barnet and High Barnet stations on the Great Northern Railway. The distinctive, well-preserved Arkley Windmill, dating from this time, is now in the private grounds of Windmill House but you will glimpse it on the walk. The village occupies part of Barnet Common which in Saxon times was dense woodland, some of which survives to this day. Despite straddling the busy A411, Arkley is a tranquil spot.

This is a mostly rural walk, which includes two lovely nature reserves. The route takes you first to St Peter's parish church, then to Rowley Green Common Nature Reserve. Next you cross an open meadow with fine views and then take a woodland path that passes the grounds of

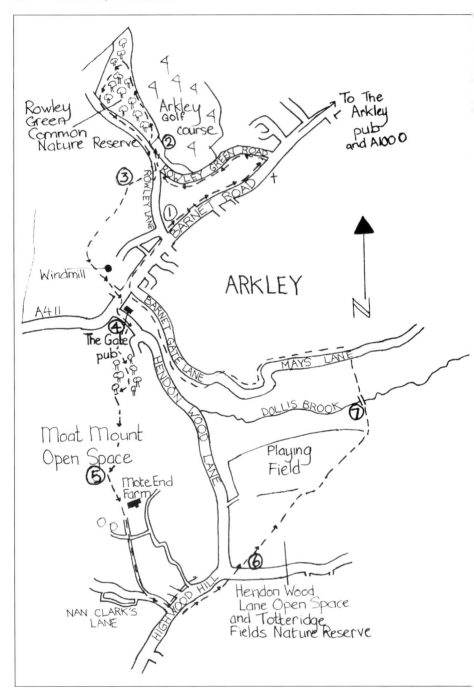

Moat Mount Open Space.

Windmill House. After a short stretch of road, you take a leafy path that comes out at Nan Clark's Lane. You return through Totteridge Fields Nature Reserve and then along the fairly quiet May's Lane.

FOOD and DRINK

The Arkley is a popular, family-friendly pub on Barnet Road, 1 mile north-east of St Peter's church. It has plenty of comfortable seating areas where children can eat with their parents, and a children's menu. There is a conservatory restaurant, and dining tables on a shaded patio. Daily specials complement a large fixed menu. Ind Coope Burton Ale, Tetley Bitter and Benskins are stocked alongside a full range of bottled beers, lagers and wines. Telephone: 0181 449 3862.

THE WALK

❶ Start by walking north-east along Barnet Road from the corner of Rowley Lane. After passing St Peter's church (1840) on the right, turn left onto Rowley Green Road and walk to Tinders Lodge at the beginning of Rowley Green Common Nature Reserve. This woodland reserve's rich and varied wildlife includes many species of birds and insects, and frogs and newts that are attracted to its bogs and ponds.

❷ If you would like to explore the reserve thoroughly, continue a little further along the road to an information board. Otherwise, turn half right and follow the yellow arrows around its periphery path. At Rowley

Lane turn left and walk back to the fork. Veer right, staying on Rowley Lane, and turn right onto the footpath signposted to Ripon Way and Barnet Gate.

❸   A little way along cross the stile in a gap in the trees on the left. Follow the path across a meadow from where there are good views of Borehamwood and beyond, to the right. Cross over another stile and go ahead along a leafy path, shortly passing the grounds of Windmill House on the left. At the end of the path continue ahead, passing Hadley Football Club on the right. At the T junction turn right onto Barnet Road, cross over and pass the Gate pub named after an adjacent tollgate, the posts of which remain. Turn left onto Hendon Wood Lane.

❹   A little way along turn right, ascend the steps and go through a kissing gate onto the footpath signposted to Barnet Gate Wood, Mill Hill and Moat Mount Open Space. Take the first left, just before the next kissing gate, and continue ahead. At the T junction, turn right, following a Dollis Valley Greenwalk arrow. At the next T junction turn left, following a London Loop arrow. Continue along this path, passing through four more kissing gates and still following the London Loop arrows.

❺   After going through yet another kissing gate turn left onto a farm track (leaving the Dollis Valley Greenwalk and London Loop routes). At the end continue ahead across the tarmac, passing Mote End Farm on the left. Cross over a stile and continue ahead, passing two ponds that the owners of the property use as a swans' refuge. On the left is Wilberforce Woods, the site of Hendon Park where William Wilberforce lived, 1826–1831. At the T junction turn left onto Nan Clark's Lane and then left again onto Highwood Hill. A plaque on the wall on the left notes Wilberforce's residence. Continue ahead, crossing over to walk along the pavement on the right.

❻   After passing Hendon Wood Lane on the left, cross back over the road, turn left and go through a kissing gate into Totteridge Fields Nature Reserve which has a rich variety of grasses, flowers and insects; look out for the red six-spot burnet moth which is active in daylight. Follow the footpath signposted to Barnet diagonally across the meadow and cross a wooden footbridge. Continue ahead to the corner of the next field and, just after a yellow arrow, cross a stile to a playing field. Turn right and follow the field boundary to turn right onto a path with a Dollis Valley Greenwalk arrow. Go down the steps, through a kissing gate and fork left.

❼   After the next kissing gate fork left and cross a wooden footbridge over Dollis Brook, following a yellow arrow (leaving the DVG route). Cross a stile then head across the field to cross another stile by a water trough, and then continue ahead to a stile in the right-hand corner of the field. After this stile turn left to walk along May's Lane which becomes Barnet Gate Lane. Eventually, after a bend in the road, walk along the footpath on the left that runs parallel to the road. At the T junction with Barnet Road turn right to complete the walk.

MONKEN HADLEY

Length : 3 miles

Getting there: Barnet High Street is part of the great North Road (A1000). Underground: High Barnet, then buses 324 and 326.

Parking: There is a car park at the eastern end of Bakers Hill (near point 6), or try streets around the green.

Maps: Street atlas, or OS Pathfinder 1140 Barnet & Enfield (GR 246971).

Hadley Green is a huge village green of sweeping meadowland dotted with graceful willows, and no less than five ponds. Its fine Georgian houses and peaceful streets give little clue that it was a place of slaughter – the Battle of Barnet, where the forces of Edward IV defeated those of Henry VI in the Wars of the Roses in 1471 and the Earl of Warwick ('the Kingmaker')

was killed, having unwisely changed sides a little before. Edward IV went on to win final victory at the Battle of Tewkesbury, entering London and killing Henry VI within weeks.

The village is built around Hadley Green which flanks both sides of the Great North Road. A hamlet existed here in Saxon times and the name derives from the Saxon

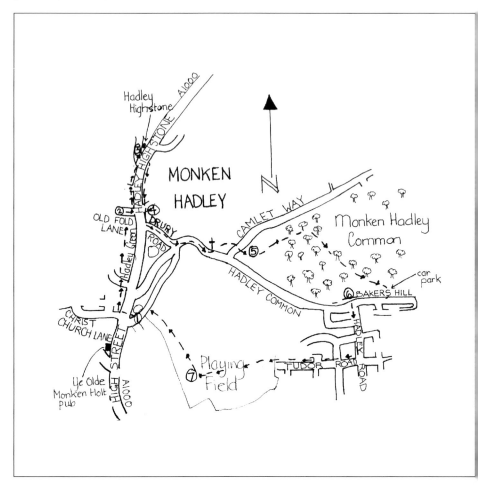

Hea-leah which means high place; the 'monken' part derives from 1139 when it was given the Abbey of Monken. Its subsequent development was due to Barnet being the first major stagecoach stop on the road north, as well as its high elevation, which was regarded as healthy.

Monken Hadley Common was part of Enfield Chase and one of the old tollgates stands at the beginning of Hadley Road, on the walk.

St Mary's church, which also features in

the walk, was founded in the 12th century. The present building dates from 1494, although it has been restored since. The flint and ironstone tower has an unusual feature, an 18th-century beacon on the top. Called the Armada beacon, it was first lit to pass on a warning of the Spanish invasion fleet. The church has a valuable collection of church plate, some of it on loan to the British Museum.

Starting at one of the ponds, the walk proceeds north through sweeping meadow-

The memorial to the Battle of Barnet.

The drinking fountain on Hadley Green.

land to a stone obelisk, which commemorates the Battle of Barnet. It continues through St Mary's churchyard to the dense woodland of Monken Hadley Common and

ends with another stretch of meadow.

THE WALK

❶ Start the walk by the pond at the south-east end of Hadley Green at the end of the High Street. Cross over the main road at the old drinking fountain just south of the pond. At the beginning of Christ Church Lane, turn right and take the path half left which runs between a road and a ditch. After passing some willow trees on the left, cross a tarmac drive and continue straight ahead, passing a pond which is covered in water lilies in summer. Cross another tarmac drive and continue ahead along a pleasant stretch of meadow with a variety of trees.

FOOD and DRINK

Ye Olde Monken Holt, on the west side of the High Street, just south of the green, is a charming little pub with a delightful olde worlde interior. It has wood panelling and a cosy, congenial atmosphere with open fires in cold weather. In fine weather you can sit in a beer garden at the rear of the pub. Children are not allowed in the bar but are welcome in the garden. The hot meals are excellent and very reasonably priced. Beers served are Courage Best and Directors and two guest ales. Telephone: 0181 449 4280.

❷ At Old Fold Lane turn right then immediately left and walk along the main road of Hadley Highstone to the fork where the obelisk commemorating the Battle of Barnet stands. The battle site is behind the houses to the east of the stone.

❸ Cross the road and turn right to walk back along Hadley Highstone, on its east side, passing the King William and the Old Windmill pubs.

❹ Turn left at Drury Road and, after passing a green with two ponds on the right, follow the road round to the left to enter St Mary's churchyard. Walk straight ahead through the churchyard, passing the church on your left. Cross over Camlet Way onto Monken Hadley Common.

❺ Turn left and walk across the mown area and then continue ahead through trees. Take the right fork and, at the incline, follow the path between a clump of birch trees and a row of oaks, after which the path becomes a track into woods. Stay on it and where it joins another track continue ahead and downhill. Just before a plank bridge, pass an oak tree on the left, with a spectacular gash on its trunk. Cross this bridge, continue ahead and veer right to cross onto a parallel path to the right. When the slope levels out veer right to another path. Keep veering right to stay near a ditch on the left. When you reach a wide track with a ditch at both sides turn left and continue ahead and downhill. Cross over a plank bridge on the right

---

PLACES of INTEREST

The **Barnet Museum** tells the history of the local area from the Battle of Barnet to the present day. There are fascinating displays on social history and the decorative arts. The museum is at 31 Wood Street just east of the southern end of High Street, Barnet. Opening times are from 2.30 pm to 4.30 pm Tuesday to Thursday, and 10 am to 12 noon and 2.30 pm to 4.30 pm on Saturday. Entrance is free. Telephone: 0181 440 8066.

The **Bull Gallery**, High Street, Barnet, is a lively arts centre holding exhibitions of contemporary painting, sculpture and photography. It opens at 10 am Tuesday to Friday, 11 am on Saturday and 1 pm on Sunday. Closing times vary. Telephone: 0181 449 0048.

---

and turn left to continue along this wide path. At the crossroads turn right and then veer half left to cross a clearing. Cross another plank bridge to a car park, then turn right and walk along Bakers Hill.

❻ Turn left and walk through the white tollgate to Hadley Road. Continue ahead and turn right by the Hadley Hotel onto Tudor Road. Walk to the end of the road, turn half left, and follow the path downhill through grass to a dirt path.

❼ Turn right onto this path which has green and white London Loop signs. Continue along this main path which goes uphill across grassland.

❽ Go through the kissing gate to the road and turn left to return to the pond on the green.

TOTTERIDGE

Length : 3 miles

Getting there: Totteridge Village (road) is the A5109, leaving the A1000 at Whetstone. Underground: Totteridge and Whetstone, then bus 251.

Parking: If you are using the Orange Tree pub there is parking on the pub approach drive. Otherwise try the side streets around the green.

Maps: Street atlas or OS Pathfinder 1140 Barnet & Enfield (GR 247941).

There was a hamlet here as early as the 13th century. The village grew after the opening of Barnet station on the Great Northern Railway. It expanded further in the 1930s when it was favoured by the 'Newspaper barons', and remains the home of city commuters because of the Northern Line link, but it is not extensively developed and parts seem to be in deep country.

In the churchyard of St Andrew's parish church is a massive yew tree that is over 1,000 years old and has a girth of 27 feet. Yew trees are associated with churches, so a place of worship may have been there that long. The earliest record of a church on the site is an order of Pope Nicholas IV dated 1291. The nave of the present building was completed in 1791 and the tower and spire

The ancient yew tree in St Andrew's churchyard.

FOOD and DRINK

The Orange Tree pub, the present building of which dates from the 1800s, has a picturesque site set back from the road behind a pond fringed by trees. Benches and tables outside face the pond, and dogs, not allowed in the pub, seem happy to wait here and watch the world go by. Inside, there is a comfortable lounge bar and a separate Carvery Restaurant. Children accompanied by adults are allowed in the bar and restaurant until 9 pm. Filled baguettes can be obtained all day in the bar. Three course meals, including three vegetarian dishes, and a large selection of carvery and fish dishes are offered in the restaurant. Beers include Fuller's London Pride and Caffreys Irish Ale. Telephone: 0181 445 6542.

---

built in 1703 were retained from an older building. The Pepys family commemorated in a number of memorials are descended from the great uncle of Samuel Pepys, the diarist. Lucas Pepys was George III's physician. The chancel ceiling was painted by the artist Sarah Elizabeth Nicholson who is buried in the family vault near the yew tree. Other prominent members of the family in the vault are Charles, who was also an artist, Charles senior, who was an architect, and Sidney, who was a musician.

The walk begins at the delightful tree-fringed pond at the southern end of Totteridge Green. From here you make your way to St Andrew's church. You then walk along paths through a very rural landscape of woodland and meadow.

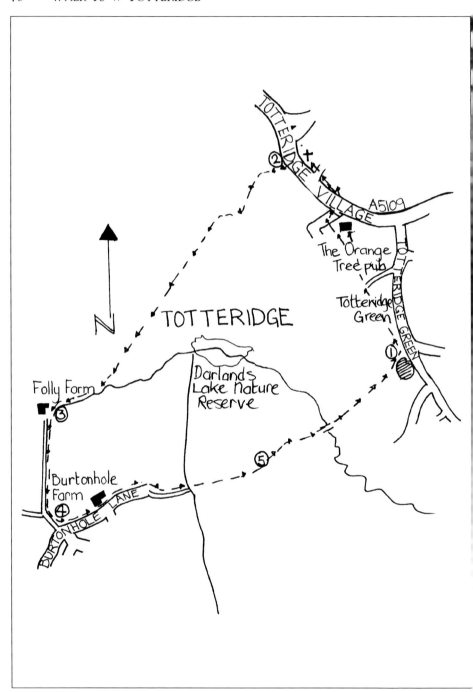

THE WALK

❶ Start the walk at the pond at the southern end of Totteridge Green (the road). Facing away from the road, and with the pond on your left, walk ahead across the grass. Just before the path ahead, turn sharp right onto a path which leads away from the pond and is parallel with, and to the left of, the road. Pass the Consolata Missionary College on the left and continue ahead. At the end of the path, just past the rear of the Orange Tree pub, turn right, cross over Totteridge Village and walk ahead to St Andrew's church. Enter the churchyard through the lychgate and walk towards the church, passing the huge yew tree on the right. After having a look around the church and churchyard leave by the lychgate and turn left.

❷ Cross over Totteridge Village (the road) and take the woodland footpath between Estrellita and Garden Hill Houses, which is flanked by a fence on the left and a brook on the right. Continue ahead and cross the footbridge over the brook, where it veers left. At the end of the path go through the kissing gate and continue straight ahead over the grass. The large building in the distance ahead is the National Institute for Medical Research. At the far side go through another kissing gate and continue straight ahead along the path with trees and a brook on the left.

❸ Where the path ends, at Folly Farm, turn left and continue ahead along the tarmac, passing the MHVSC sports ground and Finchley Nursery and Garden Centre on the right.

❹ At the crossroads turn left onto Burtonhole Lane, following red and yellow arrows. Cross over to the pavement and continue ahead, passing Burtonhole Farm on the left. At the end of the lane continue straight ahead along the bridlepath, still following the arrows.

❺ Where a red arrow points straight ahead and the yellow one points left, turn left, to follow the footpath signposted 'Totteridge'. Continue along this path as it skirts a meadow on the right. Cross a footbridge and a stile and continue along the path, still following the yellow arrow route. Go over two more stiles and continue ahead to the pond where you began the walk.

MILL HILL

Length : 4¹/₂ miles

| **Getting there:** Take Daws Lane (B1461) from the Barnet Bypass (A1). Underground: Mill Hill East, then bus 240. | **Parking:** If you use the Three Hammers pub you may be able to leave your car in the car park, but ask first. Otherwise try the side streets. | **Maps:** Street atlas, or OS Pathfinder 1140 Barnet & Enfield (GR 229925). |

Mill Hill developed after the opening of the Northern Line station, although in the 17th and 18th centuries a few large houses were built along The Ridgeway. Although Mill Hill is now spread out and suburban, this walk features the village centre which retains its traditional charm and some attractive countryside with good views – The Ridgeway is so called because it runs along the spine of a hill.

In the centre of Mill Hill's delightful village green is the Angel Pond, in summer replete with reeds and bulrushes. The adjacent High Street is said to be the shortest in London, and must also surely be one of the prettiest, with traditional cottages perfectly in keeping with the green. Overlooking the green are six

Some of the open countryside to be found around Mill Hill.

weatherboarded almshouses, built in 1696. Nearby, the Angel Cottages, dating from the 1960s, were designed by Richard Seifert, for which he won a Civic Trust award.

Just beyond the High Street, on The Ridgeway, a blue plaque on the wall marks the site of Ridgeway House, residence of Peter Collinson (1694–1768), botanist and author, who introduced the hydrangea and yucca to Britain. He planted many of the trees in the grounds of the famous Mill Hill School. Opposite is Rosebank House, a white weatherboarded building that was a Quaker Meeting House from 1678 to 1719.

Mill Hill School, built in 1807, occupies 150 acres of ground around The Ridgeway. Its main building, dating from 1825, has a façade of Ionic columns. Its architect was Sir William Tite who also designed the Royal Exchange. In a building nearby, James A.H. Murray, a master at the school from 1870–1885, prepared the *Oxford English Dictionary*.

From the village green you walk along

FOOD and DRINK

The Three Hammers on Hammers Lane is a welcoming, comfortable pub with a dining area, family dining room and a small outdoor terrace. As well as daily specials it has pastas, fish dishes, a huge mixed grill and a range of starters and desserts. Real ales served are Tetley Bitter, Burton, Pedigree and Old Speckled Hen. Telephone: 0181 959 2346.

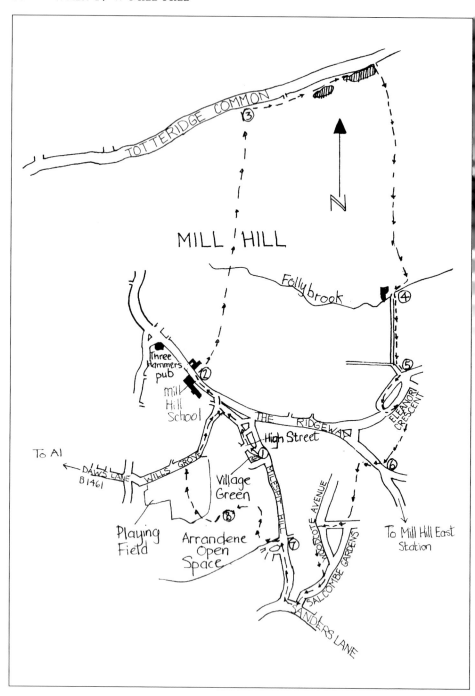

the High Street to The Ridgeway. After passing the main entrance to Mill Hill School you take a path through woodland to Totteridge Common (the road) where you walk along a pleasant wide grass verge, passing two tree-fringed ponds. This is followed by another woodland path, which, for part of the way, follows a stream. Your return is through meadowland, resplendent with wild flowers in summer, and finally across one of Mill Hill School's playing fields.

THE WALK

❶ From the village green, with the almshouses on your left, walk ahead along the High Street. Cross Wills Grove and continue in the same direction along The Ridgeway, passing Rosebank House on the right, and, on the left, the blue plaque marking the site of Ridgeway House and the main building of Mill Hill School. Cross over the road at the traffic island at the end of the school building and continue in the same direction.

❷ A little way along turn right onto a footpath through woodland, signposted to Totteridge. Staying on this path, which is a section of the Mill Hill & Totteridge Circular Walk, cross two stiles, and then continue ahead at the crosspaths. Go through two gates and over a wooden footbridge, and continue ahead to Totteridge Common (the road).

❸ Turn right and walk along the broad grassland by the roadside, passing two ponds. At the end of the second pond turn right onto a path with a high wooden fence on the left; yellow and red arrows

---

PLACES of INTEREST

The **Jewish Museum**, 80 East End Road, Finchley, London, N3, houses a large social history collection reflecting the diverse roots and heritage of Jews in Britain. It includes tape-recorded memories, a Photographic Archive and a wide range of documents and artefacts. Changing exhibitions are also featured. Opening times are 10.30 am to 5 pm Monday to Thursday, and 10.30 am to 4.30 pm on Sunday. There is an admission charge. Telephone: 0181 349 1143.

Also on East End Road, **The Stephens Collection**, at Avenue House, has displays of writing instruments, and chronicles the history of the Stephens Ink Company. Henry 'Inky' Stephens, son of the company's founder, bought Avenue House in 1874, and built an adjoining laboratory where he carried out research on inks. Avenue House is open 10 am to 4.30 pm Tuesday to Thursday. Admission is free and light refreshments are available. Telephone: 0181 346 7812.

Both museums are near Finchley Central station (Underground), one stop south of Mill Hill East station (Underground).

---

point the way. At the end of the path turn right (still following the red and yellow arrows) onto a pleasant tree-shaded path with a stream on the left.

❹ At the end of the path turn left onto the tarmac and continue straight ahead, passing Finchley Nursery and Garden Centre on the right.

❺ At the crossroads turn right and walk along the pavement on the left. Turn left onto Eleanor Crescent, take the first footpath to the right and continue to The Ridgeway.

❻ Turn right, cross over the road and turn left onto the footpath signposted to

The footpaths around Mill Hill pass over much working farmland.

Rushden Gardens. Turn right onto Rushden Gardens and at the T junction turn left onto Woodcote Avenue and then continue right along Salcombe Gardens. At the main road, Sanders Lane, turn right, then right again onto Milespit Hill.

❼   Turn left onto Wise Lane then take the first right, through the gate, into Arrandene Open Space. Continue ahead and, just before the tarmac path ends, take the uphill path veering right across grassland. At the fork veer left to keep to the edge of the meadow and go through a break in a hedge. Continue ahead and go through another break in a hedge. At the top edge of the meadow, before a stile, turn left and follow the edge of a meadow, with shrubbery on your right.

❽   Cross a stile and turn left onto a gravel track. Follow the track as it veers right and just before a stile on the left, leading to another meadow, turn onto a grassy path heading roughly north. Cross a stile onto a footpath flanked by shrubbery that goes through the Mill Hill School playing field. Then keep straight on through an open section of playing field, aiming for the next clump of trees. Pass the line of trees on the left for about 20 yards, then resume the footpath between the trees and continue to Wills Grove.

❾   Turn right onto Wills Grove and at the High Street turn right again to return to the green.

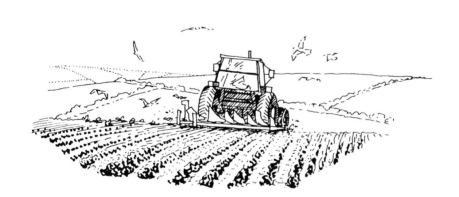

HENDON

Length : 5 miles

Getting there: From Watford Way (A41), turn north onto The Burroughs (A504), pass the town hall and turn left into Church End. Underground: Brent Cross

(near entrance to park in point 7), Hendon Central (near point 8).

Parking: There is a car park at Church Farm House, or try

near the town hall area.

Maps: Street atlas, or OS Pathfinder 1159 City of London and 1140 Barnet & Enfield (GR 229895).

The grouping of St Mary's church, Greyhound pub and preserved farmhouse at the top of Greyhound Hill/Church End gives this old centre of Hendon its village character. The church dates back to pre-Norman times; inside is the tomb of Sir Stamford Raffles, founder of Singapore. Next door to the pub is Church Farm House, a 17th-century farm house. It was opened as a museum in 1955. Special features include an 1820s kitchen. Admission is free (closed Fridays).

The walk starts from this group of buildings and then passes through Sunny Hill Park, which used to belong to the farm for pasture and haymaking. The land here is quite elevated and good views are obtained before you descend to cross the

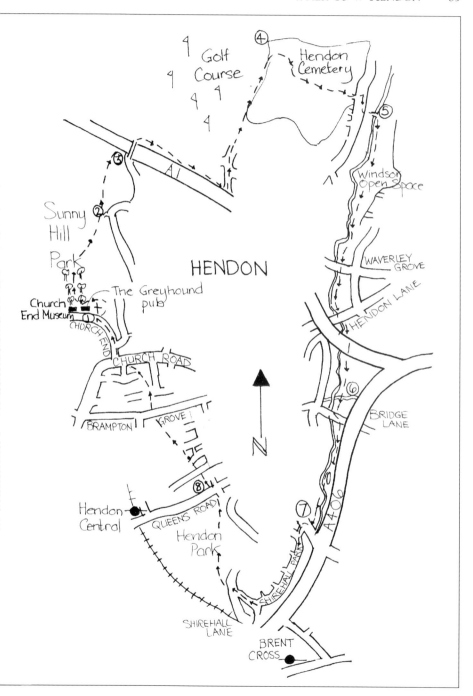

Sunny Hill Park.

A1 and walk alongside part of a golf course. Then you continue through Hendon Cemetery, which was inaugurated in 1899, one of London's first 'parkland' cemeteries and the last resting place for many members of London's ethnic communities. You continue via open space alongside Dollis Brook, whose banks are a wildlife refuge, before returning through a park and over pathways.

FOOD and DRINK

The Greyhound, next to the church, has seating at the front that makes a charming summer suntrap. It's a good place to eat, whether you want a sandwich, burger, one of the more substantial daily specials, or something off their Gourmet Menu, such as chicken in mushroom sauce or mustard pork. Abbot Ale, Flowers Original, London Pride and Old Speckled Hen are served, as well as draught Strongbow. Telephone: 0181 203 1300.

THE WALK

❶ From Church End, enter the churchyard and then turn right. Just before the end of the churchyard, turn left onto a path following the perimeter, turning left again. Pass round the back of the church, to leave the churchyard opposite the tower door. Pass behind the pub and Church End Museum. If not visiting the museum, turn right and follow the crazy paving into Sunny Hill Park. Walk along the chestnut avenue, then strike out half right across the open meadow to reach a path at the top by

St Mary's churchyard.

the backs of the houses.

❷   At the end of the row of houses, go downhill, heading half right. Go right of the cricket pitch then head towards the main road, to leave the park at the right-hand corner.

❸   Turn right and cross the A1 by the footbridge. Continue in the same direction along the minor road parallel to the A1. Take the first left, Ashley Lane, and at the end continue along the bridleway, which crosses a golf course. Keep between the sheltering trees and follow the path as it veers right through a wooded area, passing a cemetery on the right.

❹   At the end of the cemetery, enter it via the gate. Turn right to pass behind the chapel, and follow the road past the Garden of Remembrance and some of the older monuments. Follow signs to the way out and leave by the gatehouse. Cross Holders Hill Road and turn right. Just past Foreland Court on your right, turn left onto a footpath.

❺   Cross Dollis Brook and turn right. Follow the path by the brook through Windsor Open Space, a popular relaxation area in summer, part of the Dollis Valley Greenwalk, which is waymarked. Cross a road (Waverley Grove) by a bridge, and keep on under firstly Hendon Lane and then the A1, passing a weir in the brook.

❻   At the junction with another stream (Mutton Brook), keep straight on, ignoring the signs and path to the left. Cross Mutton Brook and exit Brookside Walk onto Bridge

---

PLACES of INTEREST

The **Royal Air Force Museum**, on Grahame Park Way, just the other side of the M1 from Sunny Hill Park, has an impressive collection of historic aircraft, with a special feature on the Battle of Britain and an always-popular flight simulator. Telephone: 0181 205 2266.

Lane. Cross the road, turn left, then turn right through the gates into the park. Follow the path to the right of the pond, and then between the pond and the brook. This is a haven for waterfowl. Cross a small bridge and turn right. Near the end of the park, turn right off the tarmac path onto flagstones; cross the stream and turn left, following the flagstone path by the brook.

❼   Cross the road (Brent Street), then turn left into Shirehall Park, turning left again almost immediately, then following the road round to the right. At the T junction, turn right into Shirehall Lane and cross it to enter Hendon Park. Walk diagonally through the park to leave it at the right-hand corner.

❽   Cross Queens Road carefully and take the footpath, West View, opposite. Keep straight on over Heriot Road, pass the ends of Eaton Road and New Brent Street, ignore a path to the left, pass Langley Court, cross over Brampton Grove and keep on the fenced footpath as it veers left to come out on Church Road opposite the Claddagh Ring pub. Cross at the zebra crossing and turn left. Approach the 1727 almshouses on the left and turn right into Church End. Follow this back to the start.

ENFIELD CHASE

Length : 3 miles

| Getting there: Turn westwards off the A10 at the junction with the A110. Railtrack: Enfield Chase. | Parking: There are car parks between Church Street and Cecil Road. | Maps: Street atlas, or OS Pathfinder 1140 Barnet & Enfield (GR 325966). |

Enfield Town is on the south-east fringe of what was the royal hunting ground of Enfield Chase. The name Enfield is Saxon in origin and means 'the forest clearing belonging to Eana'. A sculpture of the Enfield beast, a mythical amalgam of animals that roamed the chase, stands in front of the civic centre on Silver Street.

The Roman road, Ermine Street, ran through Enfield, which today is a lively market town rather than just another 'green belt' suburb. Enfield Palace, demolished in 1928, stood in Market Place, site of a market since the 18th century. Market House, a distinctive building with eight teak pillars, built to commemorate the coronation of Edward VII, stands where the palace once stood. Barclays Bank on the square had the world's first cash dispenser installed in 1967. St Andrew's

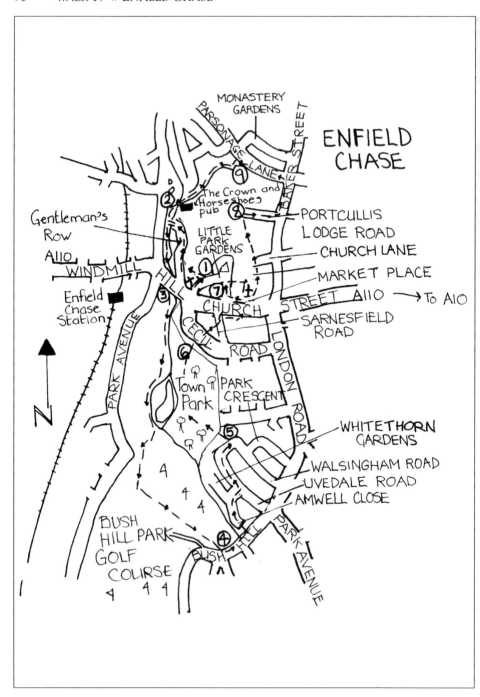

Gentleman's Row.

parish church overlooks Market Place. There has been a church here since the 4th century; the present one dates from the 13th century, although it has been

---

FOOD and DRINK

The Crown and Horseshoes pub overlooks the New River just north of Gentleman's Row. It has a comfortable bar, a restaurant and a pleasant garden at the rear. A good selection of food is on offer: sandwiches, ploughman's and grills, firm favourites such as chilli con carne and filled jacket potatoes, as well as daily specials that include vegetarian dishes, and a variety of starters and desserts. The real ales served are Abbot Ale, Boddingtons, London Pride, Flowers and a couple of guest ales. Telephone: 0181 363 1371.

---

extensively rebuilt. Inside are memorials to Sir Nicholas Raynton, builder of Forty Hall, and James Whittaker who compiled his *Almanac* nearby in White Lodge, a weatherboarded 18th-century house where he lived from 1862 to 1895.

The prettiest parts of Enfield are the streets bordering the New River, particularly Gentleman's Row which has fine 17th and 18th-century houses with gardens flanking the river, here crossed by picturesque arched, iron footbridges.

The walk takes you along Gentleman's Row, then River View, a pedestrian way of charming houses and well-kept front gardens, on the opposite river bank. You stay alongside the river through Chase Green, a remnant of Enfield Chase, regain it after crossing Windmill Hill, and eventually leave it for a leafy path through Bush Hill Park golf course. You return through the pleasant Town Park, continue to St Andrew's church and the Market Place, and then back to Gentleman's Row by another river bank path.

THE WALK

❶ From Trinity church on the corner of Windmill Hill and Little Park Gardens walk along Little Park Gardens. Turn left at the Stag pub onto an alleyway and continue ahead along Gentleman's Row, where no doubt you will want to linger to admire the houses, a harmonious and lovely mixture of buildings. Charles Lamb and his sister Mary lived in one of them, Clarendon House, from 1829 to 1833. Continue to the end of Gentleman's Row.

❷ Cross the footbridge to the east side of the New River, turn left and walk along River View, a picturesque pedestrian way of charming houses with well-kept front gardens. At the end continue ahead beside the river to Windmill Hill.

❸ Cross over the road and regain the riverside path to the left of the Data Connections building. At the fork, go right, as the left fork goes perilously near the river. When the two paths meet again, continue ahead. At the T junction, ignore the footbridge on the left and turn right onto the tarmac path through Bush Hill Park golf course. At the next T junction turn left and at the end of the path continue ahead.

❹ Turn left onto Bush Hill and go

PLACES of INTEREST

Capel Manor, built in 1752, is a College of Horticulture and Countryside Studies. Its 30 acres of grounds, which include specialist gardens, are open every day in summer from 10 am to 5.30 pm and in winter Monday to Friday from 10 am to 4.30 pm. There is an admission fee. The manor and grounds are on Bullsmoor Lane which turns off Bulls Cross (a continuation of Forty Hill). Telephone: 0181 336 4442. Nearby, on Bulls Cross, **Myddleton House** was once the home of the garden writer Edward A. Bowles. Its large historic garden contains many of the rare varieties he planted. In spring there are magnificent displays of snowdrops and crocus, award winning bearded iris in summer, and cyclamen and colchicum in autumn. Except the last Sunday of each month, and bank holidays, it is open every day from 10 am to 3.30 pm. There is an admission fee. Telephone: 01992 71771. Buses 311 and 317 from Enfield Town stop near Bullsmoor Lane.

   Whitewebbs Museum, housing a collection of vintage vehicles, occupies a Victorian pumping station on the south side of Whitewebbs Road, near Theobalds Park Road. Call 0181 367 1898 for opening times.

---

straight ahead. At Riverdale Court (a block of flats) turn left onto the footpath signposted 'Amwell Close'. When the path merges with Amwell Close, turn right onto Whitethorn Gardens. At the T junction turn left onto Uvedale Road and follow the road as it bears right.

❺ Opposite the end of Walsingham Road turn left and enter the Town Park. Turn right and then left onto the tarmac path, passing tennis courts on the left. Stay on the main path, passing public toilets, a children's playpark and a café on the right, and leave by the main gate.

6 Cross over Cecil Road and, with the library on your right, enter the small park. Follow the tarmac path as it veers right and exit onto Sarnesfield Road. Turn left, cross over the road and at the T junction turn right onto Church Street. Cross over the road at the pelican crossing and turn left to retrace your steps on the opposite side.

7 Turn right onto Little Park Gardens and right again onto Holly Walk (a narrow pedestrian way). Continue ahead, passing a school on the left and some fine old houses on the right, including the one where James Whittaker lived. At the churchyard turn right onto Church Walk and at the end, with the Market Place in front of you, turn left to enter St Andrews churchyard. Facing the south porch, turn right and follow the path around to exit onto Church Lane. Walk straight ahead, passing a car park on the right.

8 Turn right onto Portcullis Lodge Road and at the T junction turn left onto Baker Street. Pass a school playing field on the left then turn left into Parsonage Lane and continue ahead.

9 Turn left onto the footpath opposite Monastery Gardens. At the river turn right and walk along the riverside path. Just before the road turns sharp right, turn left, and cross the footbridge over the river. Turn right for the Crown and Horseshoes pub. Then turn right again and cross over another footbridge. Turn left and continue ahead to the footbridge at the top of Gentleman's Row.

ENFIELD – FORTY HALL

Length : 3¹/₂ miles

Getting there: From the A10, go west onto Carterhatch Lane, and continue straight over Baker Street/Forty Hill into Clay Hill. Railtrack: Gordon Hill (³/₄ mile	from starting point) or buses 191 or 231 from Enfield Town to Forty Hall. Parking: There is a car park at Forty Hall and one just off	Clay Hill beside the Whitewebbs Nature Trail. Map: OS Pathfinder 1140 Barnet & Enfield (GR 326987).

Just north of Enfield and the village of Clay Hill stands Forty Hall, a charming Jacobean mansion surrounded by attractive parkland and gardens. This rural walk in the surroundings of the hall and the neighbouring Whitewebbs Park takes you along pathways through parkland, woods, open meadows and the banks of a brook.

The walk begins at Clay Hill (the road) You enter Whitewebbs and Hillyfield Parks and walk through woodland to Fort Hall. You continue through another stretc of woodland, and then walk along a path b the side of Turkey Brook. The walk end with a section of a nature trail.

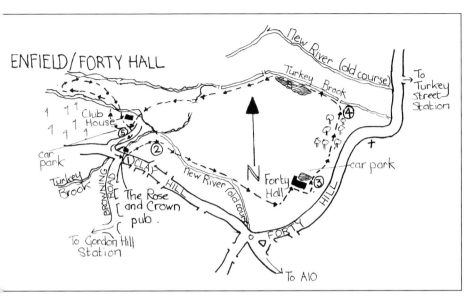

ENFIELD/FORTY HALL

THE WALK

❶ Start on Clay Hill and enter White-webbs and Hillyfields Parks to the right of the Rose and Crown. Follow the path ahead, passing a putting green on the right and a brook on the left. At the end of the putting green continue ahead into the wooded area.

❷ Just beyond a ditch, where five paths meet, turn right onto the path signposted to Gough Park. Keep on the main path and continue straight ahead, signposted 'War-

---

FOOD and DRINK

The Rose and Crown is a wonderful old pub on the edge of Enfield, dating back to 1712. It has a spacious, rambling interior with lots of wooden beams. There is a large outdoor area with benches and tables. Food is served from 12 noon to 3.30 pm. As well as a number of hot and cold dishes on a constant menu, there are daily specials. Telephone: 0181 363 2010.

---

ren Path leading to Forty Hall.' Follow the path, which eventually skirts the walled garden of Forty Hall. At the end of the path turn right to enter the garden, walk straight through and leave by the archway and iron gate. Walk straight ahead and descend the steps, go past the back of Forty Hall, turn left and continue to the ornamental lake at the front of the house. Veer right onto the tarmac then veer right again onto the pebbled path which skirts the lake.

❸ Cross over the tarmac, ascend the steps and walk straight across the car park. Take the path straight ahead through woodland.

❹ At the end of the woodland, just before a wooden bridge, take the path to the left, which skirts Turkey Brook. Continue ahead, passing two ponds on the left, after which the path has a brook on the right and a ditch on the left. Ignore the

Hillyfields Park.

turning to the left, and at the concrete footbridge on the right, continue straight ahead, passing through the metal barrier. Cross a wooden footbridge on the right, follow the path round to the left as it skirts the golf course, and continue ahead to the club house on the right.

❺   At the end of the car park turn right by two information boards for Whitewebbs Nature Trail and Whitewebbs and Hillyfields Parks. Veer left at stake 1 to follow a section of a nature trail. Keep near the trees and shrubbery on the left. At stake 2 keep straight on. At stake 3 follow the trees and shrubbery around the periphery of the meadow and eventually a brook on the left. At the metalled path turn right and

continue to the car park. Cross the car park and turn right onto the road. Continue ahead to the T junction and turn left to return to the beginning of the walk.

PLACES of INTEREST

Forty Hall, a Grade I listed 17th-century building, was built between 1629 and 1636 for Nicholas Rainton, Lord Mayor of London 1632–33. It is now a museum run by the Borough of Enfield. As well as temporary exhibitions, there are displays of 16th and 17th-century furniture, ceramics, paintings and local history, including old maps of Middlesex. It is open from Tuesday to Sunday, 10 am to 5 pm, closed Monday (admission free). Telephone: 0181 363 8196.